INQUIRIES AND SUGGESTIONS

IN REGARD TO

THE FOUNDATION OF FAITH

IN THE

WORD OF GOD.

BY

ALBERT BARNES.

"Long before positive laws were instituted, the moral relations of justice were absolute and universal. To say that there was no justice or injustice but that which depends on the injunctions or prohibitions of positive laws, is to say that the radii which spring from a centre are not equal till we have formed a circle to illustrate the proposition."—MONTESQUIEU.

" Whatever shocks or gives the least offence
" To virtue, delicacy, truth or sense
" Try the criterion—'Tis a faithful guide
" Nor has, nor can have scripture on its side
Cowper.

PHILADELPHIA:
PARRY AND McMILLAN.
1859.

NOTE.—In this Essay, the question about the actual *evidences* of a revelation is not discussed, nor is the inquiry started as to what would be proper external evidences of a revelation from God. My object did not lead me to inquire into that subject, but it has been rather to prepare the way for a proper appreciation of those evidences.

COLLINS, PRINTER.

CONTENTS.

CHAPTER I.

MAXIMS, OR SETTLED PRINCIPLES, AS BEARING ON A REVELATION FROM GOD.

CHAPTER II.

APPLICATION OF THE FOREGOING PRINCIPLES IN JUDGING OF A REVELATION.

CHAPTER III.

THE STATEMENTS OF THE BIBLE IN VIEW OF THESE PRINCIPLES.

CHAPTER IV.

THE

Foundation of Faith in the Word of God.

CHAPTER I.

MAXIMS, OR SETTLED PRINCIPLES AS BEARING ON A REVELATION FROM GOD.

§ 1. *There is such a thing as truth.*

Truth may be regarded as comprising two things:—

(*a*) Truth considered as *spoken—stated—represented;* that is, as exhibited either by words, by signs, by pictures, or by statuary. In this sense, and as the word is commonly employed, truth is *the representation of things as they are.* Thus we say of a painting or a poem, that it is "true to nature." A painting, in this sense, is true if it is a proper representation of a landscape, a water-fall, an historical scene, or of the human countenance. A drama is true if it correctly represents human nature, or is a just delineation of the passions of men. Astronomical truth is a correct representation of the heavenly bodies; botanical truth, a correct representation of plants; geological truth, a correct representation of the world before the creation of man as disclosed by fossil remains; historical truth, a correct representation of events as they have occurred in past ages; mathematical truth, a correct representation of facts in regard to number and quantity; metaphysical truth, as the phrase is commonly understood, a correct representation of the nature and operations of the human mind. In all these, and in all similar cases, the essential idea is that of a representation of things as they *are*—not as we might imagine them to be; and not as made better by leaving out offensive or incongruous parts, but as they actually *are*. In this respect, it makes no difference in what *mode* the representation is made; whether by words, by painting, by sign, by symbol, by metaphor, or by plain didactic statement. If the representation conveys to the mind a correct idea of things as they are, that representation is *truth*.

(*b*) Truth considered as found in the reality of things, or in the events and facts which are thus represented, or which lie at the basis of the representation. This sense of the term is less common than the other, and yet it is plain that this idea is included in the full notion of truth. In all truth there is not merely a *representation*, but there is a *basis* for the representation, or something on which the representation is founded, and to which it must conform. Thus, if the statement is made that two and two make four, or that all the angles of a triangle are equal to two right angles, the *statement* of these facts is truth *as represented*, but there *is* truth as the basis, or as the foundation of the statement; or, in other words, it is a *fact* that two and two make four, and that all the angles of a triangle are equal to two right angles. These facts or realities remain the same whether there is any representation of them or not; whether they are known or not;

whether they are thought of or not; whether the representation be made by words, by signs, or by symbols—in the language of a vision, or on a blackboard. And, moreover, these facts remain the same though there should be a *false* representation of them: for, if it should be said that two and two make five, it is still a fact that they make but four; if it should be affirmed that all the angles of a triangle are equal to three or more right angles, it is still a fact that they are equal to two; and this fact will remain the same forever.

These facts make it certain that there *is* such a thing as *truth*—truth in the reality of things, or as the basis of a representation—and truth *as* a representation. Truth is not arbitrary, fluctuating, vacillating; truth is not the subject of creative power; truth is not capable of being changed *by* mere power: for *no* power could make two and two equal to seven, or the angles of a triangle equal to four right angles; and no power could make such a representation conformable to truth.

It is not needful to inquire *how* it is that things come to be true. All that is affirmed is, that there *is* such a thing as truth, and that this is of such a nature that it cannot be changed by mere power or will.

§ 2. *There is that in man which responds to truth, or which is a just ground of appeal in regard to truth.*

The human mind is so made as to perceive truth, or to receive an impression corresponding to its nature; to be affected by it *as* truth. It is so constituted that an impression is made upon it by truth different from the impression made by error. It is so constituted that it may be an element of calculation in endeavoring to influence others, that they may be, and will be, affected by truth if it is fairly brought before their minds; so constituted that it is fair to presume that there will be a *uniform* result in regard to the same individual, and in regard to different individuals, by the proper exhibition of truth. In other words, in reference to the same individual, so long as personal identity remains, whether in childhood, youth, manhood, or old age, and so far as the truth produces its appropriate effect in the outward changes of life, in sickness or health, joy or sorrow, prosperity or adversity, ignorance or learning, the impression produced by truth is always the same; and so far as different individuals are concerned, the impression is the same on all. Wherever man is found, civilized or savage; whatever language he may speak; under whatever government he may live; whatever laws he may obey, or whatever form of philosophy or religion he may embrace, so far as truth makes any impression, it is always the same impression, for it always finds that in the mind which responds to it in precisely the same way. This fact, not capable, indeed, of demonstration, we always *assume* as a maxim, or as an elementary thought in our endeavors to influence others. We have the fullest conviction that, to the minds of two boys in a school, the proposition that two and two make four, conveys precisely the same idea, and that it conveys to them exactly the same idea which it will when they reach middle life or old age. We cannot doubt, also, that it conveys to those boys exactly the same idea which it did to Newton, in the maturity of his powers; or that to an American savage, to a wandering Bedouin, or to a New Zealander, it would convey precisely the same impression. In like manner, also, although we may not be able absolutely to demonstrate it, we have the fullest assurance that the impression or image conveyed to the mind by a tree, a landscape, a waterfall, a flower, is exactly the same: the same always to the individual mind in all its changes; the same to all minds, whether civilized or savage. On the same principle, so far as the minds of men are enlightened to appreciate truth, the same fact occurs in regard to moral truths. That a parent should love his child; that a child should venerate its parent; that ingratitude is base; that treachery is wrong; that to do good to others is right—all these, and similar propositions, we have every reason to suppose convey exactly the same idea to every mind. We may suppose it *possible*, indeed, that it might have been otherwise; that the eyes of men might have been so made that what to one conveys the idea of white would have conveyed to another the idea of red, and that what to-day seems to us to be yellow might tomorrow seem to be green or blue; that men might have been so made that what seems to one to be a triangle, might convey to another the idea of a square; or that what now seems to be honorable and virtuous to one, might have seemed dishonorable and wicked to another; or that, in respect to the same individual, there might have been an utter confusion on these subjects at different periods of life:—but it is evident that, in that case, the world could not have moved on at all; all would have been disorder; language would have been useless; any communication of ideas from one to another would have been impossible; society would have been impracticable; speech, schools, writing, printing, painting, statuary, would have been useless, and the world would have been a universal, though temporary, Babel, for it would soon have come to an end. We cannot advance a step in life without assuming it as a fixed principle that there is *something* in man that responds to truth; that this *something* exists in individual men, whatever changes they may undergo, and that it exists in the races in all the varieties of complexion, climate, language and art. That the basis may be enlarged by cultivation, so that new truths and beauties may be appreciated, there can be no doubt; but we always assume that there *is* a basis, and that if the truth can be brought into contact with the mind, it will always find something there which will respond to it, and that it will always make the same impression.

§ 3. *Truth depends, for its reception by the mind, on its being perceived as truth.*

The mind *sees* or *perceives* it to be true. The process of reasoning conducts to this result, when the truth arrived at is the result of reasoning; but the effect of the process of reasoning is merely to put the mind in such a state as to *perceive* that the proposition is true. When the truth referred to is an axiom, it is perceived *at once* without any medium; when it is the result of a demonstration, the process of the demonstration merely puts the mind, in reference to the truth that is demonstrated, in the same state in which it is, without any such process, in reference to an axiom or self-evident truth. That the whole is greater than a part; that if equals be added to equals the results will be equal, are propositions which commend themselves at once, without demonstration, to every mind, but it is equally true that the mind *perceives* with equal clearness, that in a right-angled triangle the square of the hypothenuse is equal to the sum of the squares of the other sides, though this is the result of a demonstration. The process of reasoning in the case has put the mind simply into a condition to *perceive* the truth of that proposition; if it has not done this, it has accomplished nothing.

In illustration of this, it may be remarked that it is possible to conceive that the power of perceiving truth as intuitive, or without the aid of reasoning, might exist to almost any extent even in created beings, as it exists in an absolutely unlimited extent in God. We may suppose that there might be, and perhaps actually may be now, created intelligences to whom all that is now perceived by men of the highest order of intellect as the result of the profoundest analysis, may be seen to be true at a glance, and may be, in fact, to their minds, *maxims*, or self-evident truths, lying, in their investigations, at the foundation of a vastly higher method of reasoning than is possible as yet to man, and bearing the same relation to a system of truth which is not now conceivable by us, which the maxims of geometry do to the highest forms of mathematical reasoning known among men. It is said of Newton that he read the propositions of Euclid as if they were maxims or self-evident truths, as being too plain and obvious to need demonstration. Even the celebrated forty-seventh proposition of the first book he did not pause to demonstrate, for he saw at a glance the truth of the statement in that proposition. Thus, too, in the ordinary occurrences of college life, we see the same fact illustrated. One member of a class, endowed with superior mathematical talent, sees a proposition to be true almost intuitively, while perhaps his fertile mind will suggest half a dozen methods of demonstrating the truth of the proposition equally as conclusive as the one which is laid down in the book before him; while another shall exhaust all his resources in mastering the train of reasoning suggested in the book by which the proposition is supported. In either case, however, the proposition, if believed, is *seen* to be true. The mind looks directly at the truth of the statement; in the one case intuitively, in the other by the aid of that which has made one step after another clear, until light has broken on the very truth to be demonstrated—as the stars of heaven guide the mariner along from point to point over the ocean, until, the stars that guided him forgotten, he sees with his own eyes the cities and hamlets and green fields of the land to which he sails. The statement here made is, that the mind perceives truth—perceives it as it is. It does not rest on the mere reasoning, but on the truth itself as now commending itself to the mind *as* true. The mental conditions which illustrate this are such as these: (*a*) There are simple, elementary truths or maxims which commend themselves to all minds, even to the minds of children, and which lie at the basis of all correct reasoning. (*b*) There is a process of reasoning based on those elementary truths, by which we are led to see some truth which would not have been plain to our minds without such aid. (*c*) There are some minds, like that of Newton, which, in the ordinary demonstrations of truth, do not need even such aid, but which start where most men leave off, assuming for themselves as axioms what to most men would be arrived at only as the result of labored reasoning. (*d*) There *may be* minds to whom the highest discoveries, even of Newton, would be perceived at once to be *axioms* or *self-evident* truths, from which they would start off on a higher career of reasoning than would be possible for any intellect now known to us. (*e*) And there is the mind of God, high above all, to whom *all* truth is self-evident; the mind of One who sees all truth as we perceive the simplest axioms of geometry, who never *reasons*, but sees and states things at once as they are.

§ 4. *There is a distinction between right and wrong, and this distinction is founded in the nature of things.*

The amount of this remark, which to most minds would appear to be self-evident, is, that a thing cannot be *both* right and wrong at the same time; or now right, and now wrong, as the result of appointment; or made right or wrong by mere will. An object cannot be black and white at the same time; or now white and now black, as the result of appointment; or made white or black by mere will. That cannot be made right to-day, which, in precisely the same circumstances, was wrong yesterday; and that cannot be right for one class or order of beings, which, in precisely the same circumstances, would be wrong in another. A lie cannot be truth, nor the truth falsehood; honesty cannot be fraud, nor fraud honesty; love cannot be hatred, nor hatred love: and as these cannot be transmuted into each other, so by no authority can they, in precisely the same circumstances, be made obligatory in one case, and prohibited in another. What is true, also, in this respect in regard to man, is true in regard to God. No one can believe that *justice* in God depends on his mere will, or that it would be proper for him to perform any act which he chose, and to call it justice at his pleasure. In like manner, no one can believe that *truth* in God depends on will, or that it would be proper for him, as an act of will, to make any statement which he chose, and to call it truth; or that it would be right to-day to call one utterance truth, and to-morrow to call it falsehood. Every man is so made as to feel assured, whatever theory he may defend that would seem to imply the contrary, that God determines to do right because it *is* right; to speak truth because it *is* truth; to be equal and impartial in his administration, because it is right and proper that he should be so. And every man is so made that he *cannot* believe the contrary; or that, under any circumstances, it would be proper for God to *reverse* things in such a way that it would be right for *Him* to do what he now denounces and condemns as evil, false, and wrong, or that the mere act of his doing it would make it right. In no conceivable circumstance can the mind of man take in the idea that it would be proper for God to give to man a wholly false representation of things; to do himself that which he has forbidden men to do; or to require of men, as an act of virtue, that which he now denounces as sinful and wrong. Every idea which we can form of the Supreme Being always implies this, that by his own eternal nature, he *is* just, and holy, and true, and good; not that he has *made himself* to be just by an arbitrary act. The mind of man, at all events, has been so made that it *cannot* take in the contrary idea, that he could have made the reverse of that which he has declared to be holy, true, good, and just, equally holy, true, good, and just; and this fact is a proof, since God made that mind, that there is that in the nature of things which is right and true. What is right and true to day was right and true yesterday, and will be forever.

It is to be admitted, indeed, that there are things which are, in themselves, indifferent, and which may be, therefore, subjects of command or prohibition. Whether one shall, or shall not, eat a certain article of food; whether he shall or shall not spend a portion of his time in a certain manner; whether he shall or shall not devote a portion of a weekly income to a specified use, may properly be the subject of command, and may, therefore, be *made* right or wrong according to the command. At the same time, however, in regard to even these, it can never be a matter of indifference whether man shall or shall not obey God when his will is made known, nor is it possible to conceive that it *could* be made right for him, in respect to these things, to disobey God. In the nature of things, obedience to the will of God is right; disobedience is and must be wrong. *Why* this is so will be seen in another part of this Essay.

In reference, also, to those things which are in themselves indifferent, and which may, therefore, be the subject of an arbitrary prohibition or command, the following principles are plain, and are such as must be admitted by all men:—

(*a*) Such a command or prohibition will not violate any *known* principle of right. It will not sanction an act of injustice, falsehood, or fraud. It will not set aside the eternal principles of truth and equity.

(*b*) It will violate no law of our nature. It will not command a father to *hate* his children, or children to hate a father; it will not require us to turn away with coldness from the suffering, the oppressed, and the sick; it will not authorize cruelty, treachery, and falsehood, for these are unchangeable principles in our nature which must have had their origin in God, and in his sense of what is right, and no mere act of will can change them or set them aside.

(*c*) In reference to *constituted* relations—or relations which do not exist in the nature of things—the same essential principles must prevail. So far as those relations are to be regulated by law, the following principles must and will be found in all acts of a correct legislation. (1.) The legislation will be according to the *design* of the relation, or the object which was contemplated in constituting the relation. (2.) It will be in accordance with settled and established principles of justice and right. That will not be made right in this relation, which is wrong elsewhere.

(*d*) The legislation will be that which is best adapted to secure the object of the relation.

There are numerous relations constituted which do not exist in the nature of things, or by any absolute necessity of nature. Yet *in* these relations, wrong will not be made right, or right made wrong; good will not be made evil, or evil made good.

§ 5. *There is that in man which responds to the distinction of right and wrong.*

This proposition is almost too plain to admit even of illustration. All men instinctively act on it in their treatment of others; all legislators assume it to be true; all parents regard it as indisputable in their treatment of their children; all authors who write on the subject of morals take it for granted; and all preachers of the Gospel make it the ground of their most solemn appeals and most earnest exhortations. As we always assume it to be true that men can be reasoned with, and can be made to see the force of argument; that a landscape will appear beautiful to the eye, and that melody and harmony will be attractive to the ear; that men are capable of friendship, and that there is that in the human soul which may be made the basis of most enduring affection—so we assume it to be true that there is something in man which will recognize a distinction of right and wrong; which will perceive the beauty and the claims of the one, and which will turn from and hate the other. Even the man who would lead us into the paths of error and sin does not base his hope on the fact that error is a thing that ought to be chosen, or that wrong is a thing that ought to be done, but he labors to convince us that the one is truth, and that the other is right, or to lead us into sin, contrary to our convictions of what is right and true. The great Tempter approached our first parents, not on the presumption that there was nothing in them which would respond to the claims of right, or that there was no power of recognizing the distinctions of right and wrong, but with the hope that he might either convince them that the evil which he proposed was, in the circumstances, right, or that he could induce them to *do* wrong, knowing that it was wrong.

It is not asserted by the remark which is now made, that there is ability in man, without teaching, or without an external revelation, to *ascertain* what is right and true, but only that there is that in man which *responds* to the distinctions of right and wrong. It is impossible to see how an appeal could be made to man on any moral subject, unless this was assumed; or how even a revelation could be of any value, unless there was some such faculty in man. We may ask, for illustration, what would be the use of submitting an *argument* to a man, unless it was assumed that there was a rational faculty which would respond to it when it was fairly brought before his mind? what would be the use of exhibiting a beautiful painting to the eye, if there was not some power in the eye to perceive colors, or in the mind to appreciate beauty? what would be the use of the beautiful arrangement in regard to music—the laws of vibrations in the air by which the notes of the octave are produced—unless there was an ear to receive such sounds, and a soul to appreciate such harmony? In all these cases we assume that there *is* an arrangement in the soul which *responds* to that which is designed to impress and affect man; and with the same certainty we assume, in all our attempts to influence others by argument, that there is that in man which *responds* to the appeals of truth and right.

§ 6. *A revelation from God will not contradict any truth, however that truth is made known.*

This, too, may be assumed as an axiom that commends itself at once to the mind; and this can scarcely be made plainer by any illustration. "*All* truth is from the sempiternal source of light divine." One truth cannot contradict another, as one duty cannot conflict with another.

The following subordinate thoughts may be suggested here as undoubtedly true, or as following from the maxim now under consideration:—

(*a*) A revelation will not contradict its own teachings; that is, it will not deny in one place what it affirms in another; or will not state as a doctrine in one place what is a palpable contradiction of what is stated in another. He to whom a pretended revelation is submitted, to be received by him, has a right to demand this; he who urges its claims on mankind is bound to show that this is so.

The remark here made is, that in a true revelation there will not be a *contradiction;* that that will not be stated in one place to be true which is denied in another; and that there will not be two statements which are not *susceptible*, by fair construction, of being reconciled, or which cannot be shown to be consistent. It cannot, indeed, be demanded that we shall be able to show HOW the one can be reconciled with the other, for there are numerous cases in science where it is impossible to show *how* two facts can be reconciled with each other, though there can be no doubt as to the certainty of each of the facts taken separately; but it may be demanded that there shall not be one statement which can be *demonstrated* to be wholly irreconcilable with another statement in the book. It could not be required, for instance, if those were doctrines of revelation, that we should be able to show HOW matter may be infinitely divisible, or HOW two lines may approach each other forever, and never meet; but it might be required that we should be able to demonstrate that this is not absurd, or that it is not impossible that this may be true; or, more to our point, it might be required that it should *not* be affirmed, in one place, that lines so produced *would* meet, and in another place that they would *not;* or that it should not be affirmed in one place that matter *is* infinitely divisible, and in another that it is *not*.

(*b*) A revelation from God will not contradict *scientific* truth.

This proposition is so plain, also, that it could not be made more clear by any demonstration. No revelation from God *could* make an affirmation that two and two make seven, or that all the angles of a triangle are equal to three right angles. If a pretended revelation should affirm such a thing to be true, men would at once, of course, reject it. It would be impossible to demonstrate that such a pretended revelation was a real one; and however strong the external arguments in favor of such a pretended revelation might *appear* to be, mankind would feel assured that there *must* be some mistake in the evidence.

What is affirmed here must be true also of *all* scientific truth. As the universe must have one author; as there cannot be independent sovereignties in the universe, so that that would be true under one form of administration which would be false in the other; as there cannot be different departments under the one great administration of the universe, in one of which that would be true which would be false in another; and as *all* truth is connected, and the facts in science must bear in numberless ways on the truth of revelation, it follows that a revelation could not contradict any established truth of science.

Three subordinate remarks, however, should be made here, which there may be occasion to illustrate more fully hereafter. (1.) One is, that the propositions which are affirmed to be scientific truths *should be such.* It should be settled that these *are* truths. There are many things affirmed in the sciences which are not yet demonstrated to be true, though they *may* be true; and there are many things affirmed which time and more full investigations may demonstrate to be false. All sciences, in their beginning, have many things attached to them, and affirmed in them, which a more full comprehension of the subject demonstrates to have no proper place in them; and before anything can be definitely asserted of the bearing of science on a proposed revelation, the scientific truth itself should be placed on a sure basis, and the different parts of the science properly adjusted. (2.) It should be made clear that the proposed revelation actually *makes any statement* on that subject, or utters *anything* in regard to it. The main purpose of a revelation, in fact, is not to teach science; at least it will not be pretended now that such a purpose is a distinct one in a revelation, though it *might* have been—for there is nothing in the nature of things which would have made it impossible to communicate all the truth now known in regard to astronomy, anatomy, botany and geology in a revelation. But such, it will now be admitted, was not the purpose of any revelation, for it seems to be assumed that these things, so far as needful to be known by man, lie within the proper range of his own faculties, while revelation must have reference mainly to things which lie beyond the compass of his natural powers. The truths of science, therefore, if taught or if alluded to in a revelation, it is to be presumed would be communicated only accidentally, and by the way, and the statement made must be regarded and treated as all *obiter* statements are made, and interpreted *as* statements incidentally made, or made *by the way;* not as forming the direct *teaching*

3

in the case, and, therefore, as not affecting the main doctrine which it was designed to communicate. If a statement is made it should, indeed, be *true*, and the friend of the revelation may be required to show that the statement is not false; but it may be properly required that it should be clearly proved that the author of the revelation *meant* to make any affirmation on that subject. It *may be* that he only used the common language of men when speaking on that subject, without intending either to affirm or deny the correctness of that language. (3.) Proper allowance must, therefore, be made for this consideration that, as the purpose of revelation is *not* to disclose the higher truths of astronomy, geology, botany, anatomy, and the kindred sciences, it would be natural that the allusion made to them, if any should be made, would be *according to appearances*, or as things *appear* to the mass of men, and in the language which men commonly employ. Thus, for example, in speaking of the sun, if there were any occasion to allude to it, it would be most natural to expect to find in the revelation such language as occurs in common life, and even among astronomers, when they speak of the sun as *rising* and *setting*, and not language which could be adjusted to the truths of the Copernican system, and which would be strictly and literally accurate. If this course were *not* adopted, two things would follow: One, that in order to strict accuracy, the highest scientific truths on these subjects should be revealed if there was any occasion to allude to the subject, which, as we have seen, would be contrary to the intention of revelation; the other, that such language to the mass of men would be, at the time of the revelation, and perhaps ever onward, wholly unintelligible; for are there any of the languages which have sprung from Babel that could be more unintelligible to the mass of mankind than would be an attempt to express all thoughts that occur to men on these subjects in language adjusted to the exactness of science? Who, in common life, could use the language which would express exactly the truths of the Copernican system of astronomy? Who could understand a man that should undertake to describe the rising or the setting of the sun, in language adjusted accurately to that system? A revelation couched in such terms would demand a new revelation to make itself intelligible to the mass of mankind.

(*c*) A revelation will not contradict historical truth. This proposition is, also, so clear that no one can call it in question. The past is fixed. Historical truths are the record of facts which cannot now be made otherwise than they are, for the past cannot be changed. The only caution that is necessary on this point, considered as a rule in judging of a revelation, is, that the facts *should be ascertained.* It should not be assumed that all the truths of history are ascertained; nor that all historical records are certainly true; nor that a mere statement by an historian, ancient or modern, however correct in general he may be, is certainly correct. Nor should it be assumed that a statement in a profane history is necessarily true, and a statement in a sacred history is necessarily false; nor that when the one may happen to come into conflict with the other, the testimony of the profane historian settles the matter against the testimony of the "sacred" historian. It may be observed, also, that nothing is more difficult than to ascertain the exact truth about an ancient historical fact. If we have any doubt about a statement pertaining to geometry, we apply the rules of a rigid demonstration, for the point relates to a truth which never varies, and where the evidence is always the same, and always at hand. If we doubt the correctness of a statement in regard to chemistry, we go into the laboratory, and appeal to the crucible and the blowpipe; if an astronomical statement is called in question, we make our appeal at once to the telescope. But nothing of this kind occurs in regard to an ancient historical fact. It is, of course, incapable of mathematical demonstration, unless it pertain to some movement of the heavenly bodies. The original witnesses are all dead, and cannot now be examined; and, in fact, they were *never* examined. The observations were made, perhaps, originally with little care, and but few of the circumstances on which the accuracy of a narrative so much depends, were stated. The historian may have made no exact statement of time; he may have misinterpreted motives; he may have been prejudiced; he may, from his point of observation, have made a report which would have been materially modified if he had had some other point of observation, and his statement may conflict materially with that of some one who *had.* In the long course of ages, also, the statement may have passed through many hands before it came to be permanently recorded, and when it was recorded it may have been under influences which tended much to increase the probability that there would be error in the statement. The historian may have also *introduced* into his narrative circumstances which he regarded as necessary to fill out the account, and to make it consistent, or he may have omitted circumstances which were really essential to a proper understanding of the case, but which seemed to him to be needless and cumbersome. It is, therefore, by no means improbable that if we had an actually *inspired* record in respect to what are now regarded as established facts in history, the existing record would be materially changed; and it is quite conceivable that an inspired and correct statement would contain many things which would be quite irreconcilable with what are now received as undoubted historical truths.

(*d*) A revelation will not contradict any *moral* truth.

This point is also clear, if it be admitted that there *is* any such thing as moral truth; or, in other words, if there is that in the nature of things which can be regarded as moral truth. If, for example, it be a correct statement in morals that a man should not utter falsehood; that he should not defraud his neighbor; that he should not steal; that he should not commit murder —if there is anything in man, or in the nature of things, which make these a matter of obligation, then it is plain that nothing in a real revelation would be in conflict with these, and with kindred principles. We cannot suppose that there is such *discord* in the universe; that there is such a conflict between nature and the God who presides over nature; that in the administration which God proposes to set up as the moral governor of the universe, there is such a discrepancy between the rules of duty revealed, and the rules of duty engraven on the hearts of men, and founded in the fitness of things, that the one would be at variance with the other. Men, therefore, do expect, and it would seem that they have a right to expect, that a revelation from God would be conformed to these well-known and settled principles, and that in a book of revealed truth, we shall find nothing that will be contradictory to truth that may be made known to us in any other mode.

§ 7. *A pretended revelation which should contradict established truth could not be received by mankind.*

This is too plain to admit of demonstration. Two opposite statements could not both be received as true. No conceivable evidence in favor of a revelation could be *stronger* than the conviction of the mind that two and two make four, or that all the angles of a triangle are equal to two right angles; in other words, it is impossible for the mind to conceive that the evidence in favor of a revelation *could* be so strong as to set these truths aside. The mind must believe them. That mind is not in a sound state which did *not* believe them.

How far it is to be admitted that truths in science, in morals, in history, are so certain as to come within this rule, is quite a distinct question; but the rule itself is perfectly clear.

The rule here referred to, embraces essentially two things:—

(*a*) If faith in a professed revelation is demanded, it is right to require that its statements shall be fairly *consistent* with all the ascertained facts of science. It could not be required that the book should *reveal* the truths of science, or, indeed, that it should make any statements on the subject at all—for the design of a book of revelation would not properly be to teach the truths of science; but it would be right to demand that, *if* any statements on the subjects of science occur as essentially connected with the doctrines of the book, or if any statements are volunteered, though not essential to the main doctrines of the book, they should be, by a fair interpretation, in strict accordance with the truths of science.

(*b*) It is equally proper to demand, on the other hand, if there is any alleged conflict between the statements of the book and the truths of science, that the facts of science shall be clearly established. It is right for the friends of such a revelation to insist, for example, that the facts in history, which are alleged to be irreconcilable with the statements of the alleged revelation, shall be clearly established *as* facts; and, in like manner, if it is alleged that the disclosures of geology are inconsistent with the statements of the book professing to be a revelation, that the facts of geology shall be clearly ascertained. The friends of such a revelation have a right to go into the fullest examination of these points, and to demand such evidence of the truth of the alleged facts as shall be sufficient to neutralize all that is urged in behalf of the proposed revelation, or such as shall demonstrate that the alleged facts cannot *possibly* be otherwise than they are affirmed to be. The science must be demonstrated; the facts must be ascertained; the contradiction must be palpable; the discrepancy must be so great that the statements cannot, by any fair rules of interpretation, be reconciled, or such that it cannot be supposed that a larger acquaintance with the subject would make it possible that the two statements should be brought into harmony. That two and two are four, and that two and two are seven, are statements which *cannot*, by any possibility, be reconciled; and if one of them occurred as the result of human investigation, and the other as the statement of a pretended revelation, they could not be reconciled; no additional light could be thrown on the subject by time; no application of any fair rules of interpretation could bring them into harmony. But the statements, for example, in the first chapter of Genesis are *not* so palpably inconsistent with the revelations of geology; the facts of geology are *not* yet so fully ascertained as to demonstrate that the two statements *cannot* be reconciled; the true interpretation of the chapter, on fair principles of exegesis, is *not* so clearly settled that it can *yet* be assumed that the *facts* in the one case may not be in entire harmony with the *statements* in the other.

§ 8. *A revelation on the same line of subjects will, so far as coincident, carry forward the truth already known —not contradict it.*

The meaning of this rule is this: that a revelation *may* make disclosures in regard to truth in advance of what is already partially known from other sources, or what will be seen to be true when the discoveries of science *come up to it;* that is, they may be such statements as would at once be seen to be consistent and proper, if, at the time when the revelation was made, all the truths which science would ever reveal were then known; in other words, that the disclosures of revelation will be in advance of, not contradictory to, the truths otherwise ascertained. The truth *may* be partially and imperfectly discoverable by reason; the revelation will not contradict the truth thus known, but will carry forward the idea, and augment the information. Between the two, there will be no more discrepancy than between the actual though imperfect knowledge of a child, and the more matured and perfect knowledge of the same child when he becomes a man; than between the lowest truths in geometry and the highest disclosures in astronomy of Newton or La Place.

An illustration of this point may be derived from the disclosures of the telescope. Vast as are the revelations made by that instrument; far as it penetrates into distant worlds; and much as it has enlarged the boundaries of human knowledge, all its disclosures are in entire harmony with those of the naked eye, and only carry forward, on the same line, what was seen by the unaided powers of vision. The telescope never penetrates into the empire of another God. It never comes into regions where other physical laws prevail than those which prevail in the worlds and systems seen by the naked eye. It never reveals any laws which are contradictory to what was before known. The properties and the laws of light, as disclosed by the telescope, in the most distant worlds, are the same with those of light on earth; and could the eye itself, now so comparatively limited in its range of observation, and to which so much of that which the telescope reveals is unknown, be so *enlarged* in its powers as to take in all that the telescope reveals, it would see things just as it does now by its aid.

It is to be presumed that the same principle will be found to prevail in a revelation from God. So far as the statements of such a revelation are on the same line of subjects which are made known to us from other sources, it will only carry forward the idea. As far as the disclosures of reason and of revelation relate to the same subject, they will be entirely the same; where revelation leaves reason in the rear, and goes forward to doctrines undiscoverable by mere reason, as the telescope leaves our unassisted faculties, and goes forward to worlds undiscoverable by the naked eye, the new truths will be entirely coincident and harmonious with those otherwise made known. Could the faculty of reason be at once so enlarged as to embrace all that is to be known in this wide field of knowledge, the same truths would be perceived, and no other, which are made known by revelation. And as, if the disclosures made by a telescope appear to be contradictory to those made by the naked eye; if it should be affirmed that the laws of light in other worlds, as made known by the telescope, are different from those in our own, we should infer that there must be some imperfection in the instrument, and should at once reject such disclosures, so man must reason in regard to a pretended revelation. He must be *assured*, if he would receive such a revelation, that all its disclosures are in accordance with the clear deductions of reason, so far as they are in the same line, and so far as those deductions go; if it should be otherwise, he must reject it.

§ 9. *A revelation will not, in its teachings, violate the constitutional principles of our nature.*

The word 'constitutional' is used here of design, and as clearly defining what is meant to be affirmed. It refers to man as he came from God; to the nature with which he was originally endowed. It is designed to distinguish this from another sense in which the word 'nature' is sometimes employed now, as referring to man, not as he *was*, but as he *is*.

Using the term '*nature*' in the largest sense, man has two 'natures;' that in which he was *made* by his Creator, and that which refers to what he has *become* by his own act; that which belonged to him as a holy being, and that which belongs to him as a sinner.

(*a*) There is the original 'nature,' or constitution, with which man was endowed. This is the most proper signification of the word '*nature*,' as applied to man; for it is that which distinguished him from all the other orders and ranks of being, as he came from the hands of his Maker. It was that which properly constituted the '*image*' of God. It is difficult, indeed, now, to determine exactly what this was; for no one in human form, save one, has ever shown, since the first man was upon the earth, what this was. We can infer what it was only from a few slight hints in the account of the creation of man in the Bible, and by endeavoring to *detach* from the idea of man all that is the result of corruption and sin, as we ascertain an ancient inscription, or an ancient figure on a shield, by removing the earth and rust which may have accumulated around it and over it.

(*b*) There is the 'nature' of man as he now is. Using the word in this sense, we apply it to man as we find him, with all his passions and propensities, as a fallen being. We speak not of his original constitution, but of that constitution as it has been corrupted by the Fall, and by indulgence in sin.

It is as such a fallen being that we are compelled now to look at man; and it is as such a being that those who write about him, and who describe him, commonly regard him. It is from this point of view that most of the books on mental philosophy have been framed; for in these man is described as he *is*, not as he *was* when he came from God. It is such a being, not a pure and spotless being, with a holy nature, as he came from God, that we see acting on the great theatre of human affairs. It is for such a being that laws are made; it is such a being that is described in the poetry and romance of the world; it is such a being that appears personated in the drama, and described in history. In no description of man in the works of mental philosophy, in history, in poetry, in romance, or in the drama, does he appear as he was when he came from the hand of God; and where a description is given of man, it is of man as he *is*, not as he *was*—a description of his fallen, and not of his original nature. The workings of his mind are not the pure workings of mind as God made it, but the workings of a mind under the influence of numberless perversities and passions, as it has been blighted and ruined by the Fall. It is unfortunate that the books on mental philosophy admit, in their descriptions of the human faculties, as part of the *constitution* of man, much that is thus the result of a lapsed state—the pervertions and accretions that have been the result of the apostasy. It is not man pure and holy, as he was when he was made, that we now see, but man ambitious, proud, sensual, covetous, envious, irritable, vain; man not with a clear intellect, but man with an intellect clouded by sin; man not believing and confiding, but man skeptical and doubting; man not hopeful and cheerful, but man desponding and gloomy; man not upright and pure, but man degraded and impure.

Hence no system of mental philosophy, considered as a description of the original constitution or 'nature' of man, has been in all respects a correct system; for none has told what man was, or what he would be, without sin. Yet, it is evident that, judging of man as he is now, we must form a very imperfect and erroneous idea of his '*nature*,' in the highest and best sense of the term; and that just in proportion as we mistake this for the original constitution of man, and allow this idea to intermingle with our conceptions of his nature, we are certain to err.

(*c*) It is to be observed, however, that, underlying all that is depraved and impure, there *are* indications of the original constitution of man, and of what may properly be regarded as his 'nature' as he came from the hand of his Maker. Even amidst all the ruins of the Fall, and all the disorders which sin has made, it is still possible to discover what the original constitution of man was; what man would be if he were wholly restored. There are accurate deductions of reason; there are just convictions of conscience; there is a moral sense which approves of what is right, and which disapproves of what is wrong. There is a perception of what is right in the relations of life; in the duties which men owe to their fellow-men; in the duties which they owe their Maker. There are things which all men see to be right, and there are things which all men see to be wrong. There is *something* in man which is the basis of appeals on the subject of morals; and there is *something* which—when the decisions of the mind are *not* prompt and clear on the subject of morals; when men are sunk in debasement and ignorance; when they seem almost to be unable to determine between right and wrong—is the foundation of a belief that they may be so elevated as to take their proper position, and discern correctly between right and wrong. We assume of the most degraded of the race that they may be raised, by redemption, to the highest attainments in determining between right and wrong; we assume that man is endowed with the faculties of reason, conscience, and moral sense; we assume that all which is necessary, in respect to these faculties, to place him in the position in which he was originally made, is regeneration and sanctification, or the restoration of the image of God to the heart.

The remark which is here made is, that a revelation will not do violence to the nature of man as thus explained. It will be in accordance with the original constitution of our minds; it will be such as will commend itself to the just principles of nature; it will be such as the conscience, under the highest teachings, and in the most perfect state, will approve; it will be such as will commend itself to the moral sense of mankind, when that moral sense is developed in the best and most perfect forms; it will contain nothing which will be contradictory to either of these things; and if a pretended revelation *did* contain that which was a contradiction of these things, it could not be embraced by mankind.

It may be admitted, indeed, and must be, that the proper limitations on this subject are not yet entirely settled, and that there is great danger, in the present fallen condition of the human soul, that they *will* be mistaken; that in forming such a judgment, what is the fruit of prejudice or passion, what results from pride, from selfishness, and from enmity to the truth itself, will be mistaken for the proper judgment of the mind, and be allowed to influence men in forming their opinion whether a professed revelation is from God. The remark now made is, that the judgment in the case *must* be founded on the clear principles of our nature or constitution as we came from God, or must be a repetition of the revelation of his will in the original constitution of man.

Thus, if in a book professing to be a revelation from God, a command were found to treat our children with neglect, such a command would be a clear demonstration that the book containing it *could* not be from God, and the race could not be bound to receive it. For there is a law of our nature as universal as any law can be—a law that reigns and rules in all lands, and that is engraved in the hearts of all men—which requires us to love our children, and to provide for them in their helplessness and dependence. No one can doubt that this is the law of Him who made man. No one violates that law without feeling that he has done wrong. No custom of society that interferes with this could obtain universal currency among men; no opinions of philosophy which denied its obligation, could be embraced by mankind. And however much savage tribes may for a time depart from that law, and whatever customs may spring up in the world that impinge on this principle, the original law will ultimately claim to be heard; that law will assert its dominion, and society will oscillate back to its true position—as, in the movements of the heavenly bodies, if there seems to be, even for the longest series of years, a departure from some great law which threatens ultimate universal ruin, the heavenly bodies will swing back again to their former position, and the universe will right itself again.* So in society. A violation of the law here referred to would tend to universal ruin. Society—the race—could not exist unless it *were* a great law that parents should love their children, and provide for their wants. The very necessities of our nature demand this, and men cannot proceed far in their disregard of the law without impinging on a great original principle of nature which reasserts its power, and restores the balance again, and brings the movements of society into harmony with the will of God.

* See a profound and beautiful illustration of this fact, as securing the "Stability of the Planetary System," in Prof. O. M. Mitchell's Lectures on "The Planetary and Stellar Worlds," pp. 163–191. Ed. 1849.

CHAPTER II.

APPLICATION OF THE FOREGOING PRINCIPLES IN JUDGING OF A REVELATION.

§ 1. *Reason as an element in judging of a revelation.*

(*a*) Reason, or our rational nature, must be one element in judging of a revelation.

This, in the nature of the case, could not be otherwise. Our rational nature, that by which, more than by anything else, we are distinguished from the brute creation, was given to us, in part at least, for a guide; and there is no subject on which we more *need* a guide than religion. It is impossible to conceive that a revealed system of religion should have no reference to our rational nature, or should make no appeal to it; that is, that in this respect a revelation should come to us as it would to an ox or a horse. God endowed us with reason, and this high endowment must have had reference to himself, to a suitable recognition of him, to his service, to the claims of his law, to the duties which we owe to him. A revelation which should profess to ignore reason, or which should claim to set aside its fair teachings, would not be received by mankind, for nothing can be more certain than that we have this endowment, and that it is given to be, in some way, a guide in everything that pertains to us.

(*b*) The great question, then, is, what is the proper

province of reason in relation to a revelation, or how far it is to be regarded.

On this point, the following seem to be clear and indisputable principles:—

1. The teachings of reason are absolute and final, in all those cases which come within its province, and where its teachings are clear. Thus, that two and two make four, and that all the angles of a triangle are equal to two right angles, are truths which are never to be set aside by any higher teaching, for they are so certain and absolute that no higher teaching could make them otherwise. God could not teach otherwise than this. He could neither affirm that this is *not* so, nor could he make it not to be so by any teaching. *How far* the teaching of reason goes, what is its province, into what fields it enters, and what fields lie beyond it, are points, indeed, that are fair subjects of inquiry; but within the proper province of the faculty, the teachings of reason are so absolute that they cannot be set aside. The whole science of mathematics evidently comes under this rule; no small part of the natural sciences; not a little of mental philosophy, and many of the truths of moral philosophy. But the proper province of reason, in respect to the point now under consideration, has never been settled, and most of the errors of theology have arisen from the fact that reason is allowed to be an umpire in matters which lie wholly beyond its proper range.

2. Reason is to be a guide in determining the *evidences* of a revelation. No revelation can be received which does not commend itself to the reason as true, or which does not furnish to the reason satisfactory evidence that it is from God. There may be other

things to which the appeal may also be made, but the evidence must be satisfactory to *this* tribunal. However much a religion may commend itself to the feelings or the imagination, however much it may do to promote the happiness of man, whatever hopes it may cherish and inspire, or however it may have been sanctioned by a venerable antiquity, it *must* have such evidence of its divine origin as to secure the assent of the highest forms of reason of which man is capable, or so that the human intellect, in its advances, can never reach a point where the evidence of its truth from reason would fail.

Of the evidences of a divine revelation reason must be the absolute judge. Whatever may be the nature of the evidence, it is competent to the reason to pronounce upon it. Whether it be miracles, or prophecy, or the doctrines that are taught, or the influence and tendency of the religion, the ultimate appeal must be made to the *reason* of mankind.

3. It is the proper province of reason to *receive* the truths of revelation when the fact of a revelation is established. Reason receives the results of evidence. It makes them its own. It embraces them as firmly as it does the self-evident truth with which a mathematical demonstration commences. The highest truths of mathematics are embraced by the mind that is conducted to them by a fair process of reasoning, with as much firmness and certainty as the axiom that at the beginning is assumed to be true, and faith in the one can no more be shaken than faith in the other. So in revelation. When reason has demonstrated the truth of a revelation, then the teachings of that revelation become just as certain to the mind as the deductions and conclusions

of its own reason, and it would as much violate the proper province of reason to reject those truths as it would to reject the plainest demonstrations of geometry. Whatever these truths may be, reason is then as much in its own proper province in admitting them and in allowing them to influence the mind in all its actions, as it is in submitting itself to the guidance of its own conclusions.

4. In points where the teachings of revelation are *beyond* the deductions of reason, then the proper province of reason is, clearly, to regard itself as subordinate to those higher teachings. It can demand only that those teachings shall not be *contradictory* to any of the teachings of reason; it cannot require that they shall not be *above* and *beyond.* The eye could demand of the telescope only that its teachings should not be *contradictory* to any of the teachings of natural vision; it could not require that its teachings should not be *above* and *beyond.* Far as it may extend the range of vision; numberless, and strange, and vast, and incomprehensible as may be the worlds and systems whose existence and laws it discloses, it can only demand that nowhere in the depths of the blue ether, in the new worlds brought to view, in the movements of satellites and comets, in *nebulæ* fixed or moving in infinite space, there shall be nothing that is *contradictory* to the laws of vision belonging to the naked eye; that the telescope shall be properly an *extension* of the range of observation, not an instrument to contradict all, or anything that man knows from other sources. With this limitation the eye greets with joy *all* that the telescope discloses respecting distant worlds. Without this, the telescope would be regarded as a deceptive instrument,

and its pretended disclosures could not be received as true.

(*c*) A material question here occurs: How far will a revelation from heaven *modify* the deductions of reason?

The general reply to this question, of course, is, that it would not in any way modify the deductions of pure and correct reason. The truths discovered by reason are truths, and no truth can by revelation be made different from what it is. No revelation could modify the propositions so frequently referred to already, that two and two make four, and that all the angles of a triangle are equal to two right angles. In reference to these, and to all similar truths, all that a revelation could do would be what is done in the higher disclosures of mathematical truths, to show the place which these truths occupy in the system, and their bearing on other truths that may be made known.

But while this is certain, it is also certain that a revelation might have an important bearing on what are *supposed* to be truths made known by reason, in the following respects:—

1. In respect to those truths in which the disclosures of reason are imperfect, or where they come short of the whole truth. Up to a certain point all may be clear and correct; beyond that, all may be obscure and dark. On that region of darkness revelation may shed a clear light, disclosing truths that man could never discover by the aid of mere reason, and where the truths already made known by reason would furnish no help, and yet all would be in accordance *with* the truths before discovered.

2. Revelation might set aside many things that *seem*

to result from the discoveries of pure reason; many things that have been derived even from correct premises. The doctrines which reason may be supposed to have discovered, may *seem* to be fair conclusions from the premises; and yet it may be true that the conclusions reached are all false. The ignorance of the true doctrine may be so real, and the region so dark, and so impenetrable by any powers of the mind, that the mind may be unable to *see* the errors, or to detect the fallacy, and yet there *may be* an error and a fallacy which it might be the proper province of a revelation to expose and remove. The mind itself might, indeed, never have detected the fallacy; it might never of itself have seen that the supposed true doctrine did not result from the premises; and yet the revelation of a true doctrine on the subject might show the error, and at the same time be seen to be more entirely consistent with the conclusions of reason than what had been supposed to be the true doctrine was.

3. All those doctrines which are the result of conclusions from wrong *principles* would be set aside, of course, by a revelation. In such cases, the conclusion might be fairly derived from the premises assumed, and yet as these premises were false, the effect of a revelation would be to set the whole aside. By a statement of just principles, the whole superstructure would fall. Thus, for example, certain forms of doctrine, extending very far, follow from the views which are taken of human nature, and the whole system, perhaps an entire system of theology, would depend on the doctrine assumed to be true on that subject. If it should be assumed that man is not fallen, that he is pure, that he has no more propensity to evil than to good,

then there would follow from that an entire system of theological views of a very peculiar character. If it should be assumed that man *is* fallen, that he is wholly depraved, that there *is* a propensity to sin which always develops itself except as restrained and checked by the grace of God, then an *opposite* system follows from that assumption, extending into an entirely different view of the whole work of saving men. In both cases, the reasoning by which the systems are supported, might be perfectly correct if the premises were admitted; in either case, the system would fall if a revelation should settle the disputed point about the nature, character, and tendency of man.

4. All those cases in which reason had been warped or perverted by prejudice, by passion, or by selfishness, would be modified by a true revelation. This might not occur in purely scientific subjects; but there is a large class of subjects pertaining to morals where the whole form of the doctrines embraced would be shaped by the colored medium through which the subject was viewed. In fact, no small part of the moral and religious systems in the world have had their origin in the heart rather than in the head; and all such would be affected by a correct system of revealed truth.

The friends of revelation, it would seem, must concede the principles laid down in this section, and the enemies of revelation have a right to hold them to these principles. The world *will* hold the advocates of revealed truth to these principles. It will be impossible to convince mankind of the truth of a pretended revelation in which these principles are not recognized, and no system in which they are not, in fact, admitted, can secure a permanent hold on the world. Circumstances might give a temporary triumph and prevalence to a pretended revelation which should violate these principles; but the nature with which man is endowed will, sooner or later, rëact, and reason will assert its proper place. It acknowledges ultimate subordination only to a true revelation from God. For its own department, it is supreme; it yields permanently only when a higher teaching, pertaining to regions beyond its proper domain, enlarges its own just conclusions, and sets aside those which are false.

§ 2. *The moral sense as an element in judging of a revelation.*

(*a*) It *is* an element in judging of a revelation. The moral sense—the conscience, the power of deciding on good and evil—is one of the original principles of our nature, found among all men, and, therefore, a part of the constitution with which man was endowed. It is impossible to conceive of *man* except as endowed with this faculty: for, in all our descriptions of man, this idea is as essential as the idea of reason. It is one of the things which separate him from the inferior creation, and which is never approached by any of the inferior creation; one of the things which assimilates man to the orders of creatures above him, however exalted, and however unlike him they may be in other respects; one of the things which give man a resemblance to God himself. As a revelation must pertain to *duty* as well as to *truth*, it is clear that there must be, so far as duty is concerned, a recognition of this faculty, as there must be a recognition of the faculty of reason, so far as truth is concerned.

(*b*) A pretended revelation could not be received by

mankind which paid no respect to this faculty, or which contradicted its plain teachings and decisions. Man is so made, for example, that he must obey his conscience. A pretended revelation which should teach that he was never to obey his conscience, or that he was to make it a rule of life to go against his conscience, could not possibly be from the same Being who has made man as he is, and who has taught him, by his very constitution, that his conscience *is* to be obeyed, and that to act against its decisions is sin. Two systems so unlike as these would be could not possibly be from the same source; and as man is so made that he can have no doubt as to his obligation to obey the dictates of his conscience, a system which should teach and enforce the contrary must be rejected by mankind. It may be laid down, therefore, as an undoubted truth, that, if a revelation could not be made to "commend itself" to the consciences of men, it would not be from God.

(*c*) A very material question, therefore, arises: how *far* this rule is to be allowed to control us in judging of a revelation, or what, if any, are the proper limitations of the rule?

1. There are things so universally agreed on by mankind as to show that they are laws of our nature, and they must be respected and confirmed, if a revelation is to be received by the world. What is the exact range of these subjects, how many *things* are included, may be, indeed, a question, for on this point, as on most others, there are *three* classes of subjects: (*a*) There are those which are perfectly plain, and which are at once seen to be right; (*b*) There are those which are with equal clearness at once seen to be *wrong;* and

(*c*) There is a middle class, a large margin, where it may be doubtful whether an action is right or wrong; or, in other words, there is a region of perfect light, a region of perfect darkness, and an extended twilight, which is neither.

An illustration of this point may be derived from *taste*. There *is* such a thing as correct taste in poetry, in eloquence, in statuary, in painting. It may not be easy to determine, in the abstract, what this is, and there may be a variety of subjects on which the tastes of nations or individuals would differ. Yet there is a correct standard of taste: a standard in accordance with which the best specimens of poetry and the arts are preserved and sent down to the admiration of future times. Now, if we were to conceive of a *revelation* on the subject of taste, we should be certain that it would accord with the general judgment of mankind. A revelation which should declare that the works of Homer were not, in the main, in accordance with the decisions of correct taste, or that the Apollo Belvidere, or the Venus de Medici, or that the Cartoons of Raphael, or the Aurora of Guido, were in bad taste, would be practically rejected by mankind. These works of art would continue to be admired in spite of the decisions of such a revelation; nor is it probable that such a revelation would make the least perceptible change in the general judgment of mankind in regard to them. In spite of the decisions of such a revelation, the poems of Homer would continue to be printed and read, Florence would be crowded with the lovers of the arts, and Rome, which has preserved so many specimens of taste, would be the resort of as many pilgrims as now. So it would be in a pretended revelation in regard to morals or religion. There is a large class of subjects on which men everywhere would act as they do now; and if such a revelation did not recognize the justness of these principles, it would be rejected by mankind. Men would recognize the obligation to be honest, to be humane, to respect their parents, to declare the truth, whatever might be the command of such a revelation, and however practically they may now disregard these principles in their conduct, it could never be possible to commend to mankind as a code from heaven—from the true God—a system of teaching which should declare that the common rules of morality are not obligatory.

2. A revelation will accord with the highest development of moral truth in the progress of society. It will not only meet the comparatively limited, though just views of morality in the primitive stages of society, and in the uncultivated portions of the world, but it will accord with the highest attainments in moral truth which the world has reached, or will reach; for a revelation must be made for all ages, and all lands. And as a revelation for the race must be designed for all times and all lands, a time never can come, and a state of society never can exist, which will be on the subjects on which a revelation is made in advance of it. It is not enough, therefore, to be able to show that the revelation is, in these respects, *up to* the age in which it was made, or that it did not contradict any of the truths then known; it must be *up to* every age, and must contradict none of the truths that will ever *be* discovered. It must be as really adapted to the highest stage of civilization, intelligence, and refinement, as to the lowest; it must as

really be *in advance* of the highest point to which society ever will come, as it was of the lowest and humblest condition or state of the world when it was given. If *not* so, then it could easily be demonstrated, that a revelation was not *necessary* for man—since in the regular development of knowledge, without such a revelation, society would ultimately come up to the point where a revelation would place the race; or, if it contained principles which were contradictory to those which would be established in a future age by the unaided efforts of the human intellect, that fact would prove that it was false; for truths, whether discovered by human wisdom, or revealed directly by God, cannot be contradictory to each other. Such a revelation as should fall behind the highest attainments of society might indeed be *useful* in the lower stages of society, until the powers of man should come up to its disclosures; but a professed revelation that should be contradictory to any of the discoveries which the human intellect could make in its highest exercise, could not possibly be from God.

3. If a revelation does not meet these conditions, it will be rejected, sooner or later, by the world. It cannot hold on its way; it cannot secure an ascendancy permanently over the human intellect, unless it is found to be in accordance with these conditions. However it may for a time secure a hold on the faith of mankind; however it may seem to promote human happiness; however it may appear to impart comfort and hope in the world, yet if it do not meet these conditions, it will sooner or later be rejected by mankind. One of the indisputable conditions on which the world is to be kept from infidelity is, that

the revelation proposed to mankind shall *accord* with the highest disclosures of truth as learned from any other source, and that it shall be *in advance* of all other disclosures in its own peculiar department. And what is true in general in this respect, is true also in detail. If the revelation teaches *any* doctrine which can be demonstrated to be contradictory to the disclosures of truth from other quarters, or if, in its own proper department, it does not contain disclosures that are in advance of what men might gain from other sources, that particular doctrine will be rejected, and a rejection of a doctrine from such a cause will drag down with it the entire book which claims to be a revelation from God. Just in proportion as a professed revelation should be found to contain sentiments, or authorize acts, or lend its countenance to institutions, customs, or laws that violate the moral sense of mankind, that are contrary to the spirit of humanity, that impede the progress of society, that cramp and fetter the human powers, that are contrary to the best arrangements in the family relation, or that tend to debase and degrade mankind, just in that proportion will infidels be made in regard to such a pretended revelation; for mankind will not receive a system as from heaven that violates the established principles of our nature. And hence it follows that all the defenders of a revelation, in proportion as they endeavor to show that it sanctions and sustains such institutions and customs, become the promoters of infidelity in the world, and are, to the extent of their influence, and the success of their arguments, responsible for the infidelity that may prevail. A pretended revelation that, by its fair teaching, sustained oppression and wrong;

that was the advocate of ignorance and barbarity; that fostered a spirit of revenge; that encouraged licentiousness, or any of the institutions that contribute to the indulgence of licentiousness; that advocated irresponsible power, or that placed slavery on the same basis as the relation of parent and child, husband and wife, guardian and ward, would so impinge on the great principles of our nature, and be so at war with the best interests of society, that the world could not ultimately receive it, and all who should endeavor to show that such a revelation *did* sustain and countenance such doctrines, would of necessity become the practical diffusers of infidelity in the world.

(*d*) It is a material inquiry, however, how far a revelation would *modify* the opinions of men as to what *is* right and wrong, or whether it should be allowed to effect any change in the sentiments that are ultimately to be employed in judging of its own claims. Is it to be demanded that it shall conform in its decisions to what is actually received among men on the subject of morals, or must it be allowed to set up a standard of its own, supposing that, however the prevailing opinions of men may differ from that, it will so commend its new precepts to what is in men that they will perceive it to be right. Will it presume on the existing moral sense among mankind, or will it create a higher and purer moral sense which will itself become the standard of appeal in the truths which it proposes for belief.

Both these things are, to some extent, true:—

1. There *is* a class of moral truths which are received by all men, and which are never to be varied. How wide the field is, and what it may embrace, it may be

difficult to define, for there is a large margin that is indeterminate and doubtful. But there *are* moral truths which are well settled in the estimation of mankind, and which are to remain so: truths which commend themselves to man as entirely and as universally as the canons of a correct taste do, or as the elementary principles of geometry, and which could never be set aside by the teachings of revelation. These truths are the basis of morals. They are found essentially in the writings of Confucius and Seneca, as well as in the Moral Philosophy of Paley. They are essential to the well-working of society, and would soon be wrought out again, and in substantially the same forms, if all existing books on morals were destroyed, and if society were to begin anew. All that revelation could do, in regard to these truths, would be to confirm them by its own authority, to separate them from errors to which they might be attached, and to enlarge their sphere.

2. But there is a much larger number of points on which revelation would be absolute. Intermingled with those truths of morals above referred to, there are many errors which it would set aside. There are local opinions and practices which have no foundation in any law of nature, and which it would set aside. There are laws of human enacting which it would supersede. There are rules regulating oppressive and unjust systems, and which are essential to the existence of those systems, which it would abolish. There are opinions and customs which are the result of ignorance, or passion, or false systems of religion, or pride of life, over which its control would be entire. All these it would abolish, and it would establish a purer morality in their place.

Yet even in regard to these, it is to be observed that it would not merely abolish them by its own absolute authority, but it would, at the same time, create such a moral sense by its influence that men would see and approve of the principles of the religion which did abolish them, or which, even if there were no positive precept in the case, would lead men of themselves to abolish those rules. Thus, in the laws, for instance, which Christianity has originated in regard to polygamy, to infanticide, to human sacrifices, to revenge, to the appeal to God by duel, it has, at the same time, created such a conscience or moral sense that the minds of men *approve* the change; such a moral sense that, in most of these instances, even if there had been no direct *rule* of Christianity on the subject, the change would have been produced by men themselves, by the silent influence of the religion in new moulding the moral sense of mankind. Perhaps it is not too much to affirm that there is no existing evil in the moral world which Christianity, by such a silent influence, if fairly applied, could not remove, even without an absolute precept; certain it is that there are none of its peculiar laws which do not commend themselves to the moral sense of men—either the original moral sense, as Christianity finds men, or the newly formed moral sense of mankind, where its influence is properly felt. Many of the evils of the world silently melt away under that influence, even where there is no positive precept; and when that religion shall pervade the earth, and shall transform the moral opinions of men and the customs of society into conformity to its own standard, it will sustain itself by its own power—by its commending itself, in all respects, either to the original moral sense of mankind—the deep, fundamental principles of our nature in regard to moral truth—or to that high and pure moral sense which Christianity will have created in anticipation of its ultimate triumphs, and as the basis on which its eternal reign is to rest.

§ 3. *Science as an element in judging of a revelation.*

The following are manifestly correct principles on this subject:—

(1) Science is, and must be, an element in judging of the claims of a revelation from God. Science is, properly, a mere statement of *truths* or *facts*, arranged into a system, and those truths or facts constitute, properly, the science. Whatever theory may be proposed in explanation of the facts, or whatever hypothesis may be adopted, the facts constitute the science, and are all for which the science is responsible. The theory—the hypothesis—may or may not be correct; the classification may or may not be perfect and complete; but the facts or truths, as far as facts and truths are known on the subject, are to be regarded as constituting the science. Thus, there are certain facts in regard to the "changes of composition that occur among the integrant and constituent parts of different bodies" (*Henry*), or to "those operations by which the intimate nature of bodies is changed, or by which they acquire new properties" (*Davy*), constituting the science of chemistry; there are certain facts in regard to the structure and functions of the human frame, to the motions of the heavenly bodies, to the structure and laws of plants, constituting the sciences of anatomy, astronomy, and botany. These are what they are, and cannot be affected by any revelation. They remain the same

whatever system of religion or morals may prevail on the earth. They could not be made different from what they are by a revelation. Better and more perfect theories, in explanation of these sciences, might, perhaps, be proposed, than those which now prevail; new facts might be brought to light, if the revelation extended to such disclosures; things which had been regarded as facts might be set aside; but the facts themselves could not be changed.

It is true that a revelation *might* be made which would in no manner come into contact with the disclosures of science on these subjects. It might be so framed as to make disclosures *only* on moral and religious subjects, and be so entirely independent of all the subjects of science that there could be no conflict, or no points of contact. But this could scarcely be expected. The world is God's own world—made, fashioned, and governed by Him; and the *facts* in relation to its creation, its history, its design in manifesting the evidence and goodness of God, are so obvious and so material, that it is not to be presumed that there would be no allusion in a revelation from God that would bear in any manner on the subjects of science.

(2) If any statements are made in a revelation bearing on the subject of science, those statements must be consistent with the disclosures of science.

This remark is to be taken in the most *absolute* sense. A pretended revelation could not be a revelation from God, if it contradicted any of the facts or truths of science. These facts or truths, as already remarked, are fixed, and are not subject to change; and a statement from God himself, who has made all things, and who knows all things, must be in accordance with those facts.

But it must be *true* science. The facts must be clearly ascertained. We cannot assume that all which has been regarded as science, or all which has been connected with the sciences as theories, or hypotheses, is true science. The friends of revelation have a right to demand that the alleged facts of science shall be beyond question, or such as are fully established; and they have a right to institute the most thorough examination of the alleged facts of science before they are called upon to meet the question whether they are or are not in conflict with revelation. In respect to this, there is occasion for more modesty and diffidence than have always been manifested by scientific men on the points where science has seemed to come into conflict with revelation. They who are best informed as to the history of science, will be among the most cautious in coming to hasty conclusions on this subject. They will remember how many theories have prevailed on each of the sciences, which have ultimately been abandoned; how imperfect science has been in past times, and how far from perfection it is now; how few of all the facts which enter properly into science have been observed, and how imperfectly nature has been analyzed: they will not be slow to perceive how wide is the range of scientific truths as contemplated by the Creator in comparison with the range which passes under the observation of the most gifted of mankind —how little, in fact, is known of the wonders of a universe which required in its constitution all the wisdom and power of an infinite God, and they will not hastily come to the conclusion that the facts are so fully and certainly known in any one of the sciences as to make it sure that longer observation, or more profound analysis, might not bring it into conformity to a statement in a professed revelation that might *seem* to come in conflict with the science as at present understood.

Further: a revelation from God will be consistent with the discoveries of science in its highest developments, or in its ultimate attainments. In other words, there can never arrive a period when a true revelation would not retain as firm a hold on the human mind as in the rudest stages of society; that is, the discoveries of science can never outrun the disclosures of revelation. As God is the author of a true revelation, and as he is the author of the world, and, therefore, the source of all knowledge, alike in science and revelation, the two must ultimately harmonize. It cannot be conceived, therefore, that the disclosures in geology, for example, will be ultimately found to be inconsistent with the fair interpretation of the book of Genesis about the creation of the world, if it be admitted that the book of Genesis is a part of a revelation from God. The unbeliever has a right to demand that at any and every stage of the investigation no one fact shall be inconsistent with a proper interpretation of the book of Genesis, and he has an equal right to demand that all the statements of the book of Genesis, bearing in any way on the subject, shall, by a fair interpretation, be consistent with the ultimate disclosures of the science.

But while this general proposition must be conceded by the friends of revelation, and the friends of science respectively to be correct, there are two remarks which it is proper to make respecting the principle:

(*a*) One is, that the investigations of science and the interpretation of the Bible should be pursued in accordance with their own proper laws, and each one irrespective of the results which may be reached in the investigations of the other. The pursuit of truth in every department should be on fair and independent principles, whatever may be the ultimate result. Facts, in the one case, should not be forcibly made to bend, nor language, in the other, in order that the one may be accommodated to the other. The friend of science should be allowed to pursue his investigations, so far as the result to be reached is concerned, with as entire independence as though there were no book in the world pretending to be a revelation—that is, for the time, *ignoring*, so far as his science is concerned, the existence of the Bible; and the friend of revelation should be held to a rigid and fair interpretation of the words of his book as though the disclosures of science were wholly unknown—that is, for the time, so far as his department is concerned, *ignoring* all the facts of science. In other words, in the laboratory, in the observatory, in the examination of fossil remains, a text of Scripture should be allowed in no manner to mingle with the revelations of the crucible, the telescope, and the blowpipe; or with the 'testimony of the rocks,' either in regard to the age of the earth, the records of former times, or the movements of the heavenly bodies. In these investigations, the question is not even to be asked whether the disclosures of science and of revelation will ultimately coincide, or whether they will be found to be contradictory and irreconcilable. That is a point to be determined *after* the investigations are all made, and all the facts are ascertained. The moment that a man of science allows a question respecting the harmony of his conclusions in science with a book pretending to be a revelation, to influence him in his inquiries, that moment the true spirit of scientific investigation has departed, for he has left the proper province of science, and abandoned an essential principle in all scientific investigations; and the moment a friend of revelation allows a consideration of this kind to influence *his* mind, and to induce him to pervert a word from its proper meaning with a view to accommodate it to some statement of science that is in conflict with the fair statement of the book before him, that moment *he* has abandoned his proper province as an interpreter of revelation.

(*b*) The other remark is, that while this is a just principle, and one to which the friend of revelation should be willing to be held, it is also to be remembered that a current and prevailing interpretation of a revelation *may be* a false interpretation, and that it may occur that while there *seems* to be a discrepancy, or a contradiction between the statements of such a book and the disclosures of science, a *true* and *fair* interpretation may be entirely consistent with all the facts disclosed by science. Nothing has been more common in the church than to affix a false interpretation to the Scriptures, and then to hold this as an essential part of the true faith; nothing more common than to persecute those who held some doctrine of science in conflict with that false interpretation, and to regard them as heretics. No small part of the persecutions which have occurred *in* the church have arisen, not from any denial of a true doctrine of the Bible, but from a denial of some opinion which was held to be a doctrine of the Bible, and which was sanctioned by the church, but which a more correct interpretation has shown to be no part of the teachings of revelation. Thus Galileo was persecuted, not for any real denial of a doctrine of revelation, but for maintaining an opinion in regard to the material universe which was contrary to the established doctrine of the church, as it was supposed to have been derived from the Bible, but which has been subsequently universally admitted to be in entire accordance with all the teachings of revelation. No man now holds that the Bible teaches the Ptolemaic system of the universe; no infidel now insists that the believer in revelation shall be held to maintain that that system is taught in the Bible. The writings of all infidels might be searched in vain for an objection to the Bible drawn from that source; and no objector to the Bible would risk his own reputation in urging such an objection.

It is impossible for any objector to the Bible to demonstrate that all the arguments now derived from the recent and as yet imperfect science of geology against the statements of the Bible, may not yet take their place with the objections which could have been urged as derived from the new doctrine of astronomy in the time of Galileo; or that the real difficulty in regard to the doctrines of geology as coming into alleged conflict with the Bible, may not be a difficulty, not in the science itself, or in the Bible when fairly interpreted, but in the *interpretations* heretofore affixed to the Bible, and received as the undisputed doctrines of the church. The process of adjustment, in such a case, will consist essentially of two things: first, in ascertaining exactly what the science *is;* and secondly, in ascertaining precisely what the Bible *teaches.* If these points are clearly ascertained, then, and not till then, will the time have come for the inquiry whether the statements of the two are harmonious. No friend of the Bible can *assume* that the alleged disclosures of geology in regard to the duration of the world, and the history of extinct races of animals, are false; and no geologist can *assume* that the interpretation affixed to the Bible hitherto in the church is the true one, and that he has overthrown the authority of the Bible when he has shown that the disclosures of geology are contradictory to that current interpretation. Such assumptions, in regard to astronomy, would have determined nothing in the time of Galileo; such assumptions in regard to geology would determine nothing now. It is still quite competent for the friend of the Bible to rëopen the question as to its meaning; and he should be allowed, in respect to the disclosures of geology, and to all other sciences, as in the case of the revelations of the telescope, the most ample opportunity for instituting the inquiry as to the fair interpretation of the book which he regards as a revelation from God.

(3) If it be asked, then, how far the teachings of a revelation from God would modify the teachings of science, the following remarks will furnish a correct answer to the inquiry:—

(*a*) Such a revelation will in no way modify the *facts* of science. These are what they are: they are what are disclosed as such by the fair application of the principles of scientific investigation. They are not to be set aside—they cannot be set aside, by any revelation from heaven. The friend of revelation is not to require that they shall be set aside or rejected. He is not in any way to ask that they shall be modified, or that their disclosures shall be made to bend to the teachings of the book which he regards as a revelation. He is to admit them to be true, whatever may be their bearing on the book which he regards as a communication of the divine will. He is to allow every fair statement in regard to such disclosures, and every fair inference from them. He is to suffer them to strike where they will, and whatever may be the effect on the system which he holds.

(*b*) On the other hand, he may insist on two things:—

He may demand that the facts of science which are alleged to come into conflict with the teachings of revelation shall be fully ascertained. They must not be fancy, theory, conjecture, nor must a conclusion, unfavorable to revelation, be drawn from them where they are imperfectly developed. He may urge this point to the utmost; he may demand the most rigid demonstration of the truth of the facts that are alleged to be in conflict with revelation, and may insist on a suspension of the judgment until the science shall be settled and clearly understood.

He may, also, insist on the privilege of re-examining the interpretation of the book of revelation, and institute the inquiry whether the interpretation which has been affixed to the book is the true interpretation, and whether, in the fair use of language, the teachings of the book may not be consistent with the teachings of science. That was the point where the church should have paused in the case of Galileo, and that may be demanded now. The friend of science should concede that as a true principle; the friend of revelation should admit that if, after the fullest and fairest inquiry, the two cannot be made to harmonize, the book which he has regarded as a revelation cannot be from God.

CHAPTER III.

THE STATEMENTS OF THE BIBLE IN VIEW OF THESE PRINCIPLES.

THE principles which have been laid down in the preceding chapters are such as, it must be presumed, will commend themselves to all men; and they are undoubtedly such as the world will act on in determining the claims of a pretended revelation from God. If a book should now for the first time be published to the world, asserting a claim to be a revelation from God, it would, beyond all doubt, be subjected to these tests; and if the book now received by the Christian world as a revelation from God is to retain the hold which it now has on the human mind, and is ultimately to obtain a universal belief among mankind that it is from God, it must be shown that it meets the demands implied in the principles which have been stated.

One of the most important inquiries, therefore, before the world, is whether the Bible does, in fact, meet these demands. This inquiry is practically suggested in all cases in which the Bible is proposed to man as a guide to heaven; it comes before the minds of men in all scientific investigations; it is publicly asked by avowed sceptics, and it is secretly before the minds of multitudes of men who have no desire to be known as sceptics; it is always asked when new discoveries in science are submitted to the world, and it enters into all the inquiries about what the Bible sanctions or disapproves in morals. Whenever and wherever it is alleged by the friends of the Bible that it declares that to be truth which the scientific world declares to be false; whenever and wherever it is alleged that it authorizes a course of conduct which the world has pronounced to be wrong, just so much is done to create and sustain infidelity: to throw off, on the one hand, one class of men, and on the other, another, and to render it impossible to convince either that the book can be from God. Perhaps a more essential service, therefore, could not be rendered to the cause of truth, than by the inquiry whether the Bible, according to the principles laid down in the previous chapters, does commend itself to the world as being in accordance with the ascertained facts of science, with the fundamental laws of our nature, and with the convictions in regard to right and wrong which God has enstamped on the human soul.

This might open a very large field of inquiry, for it might lead to an examination of all the historical statements, all the statements on the subject of morals, and all the statements that have any bearing on the subjects of science, to be found in the Bible. Few men would be competent to such an examination; and yet, if a man were competent to it, it may be doubted whether he could perform a more important service for the world than by such an examination. There are few more inviting fields, now unoccupied, for a man who would wish to render a valuable service to the world, than this. The world has not *yet* furnished the man that is qualified for this: the man who should combine in himself the highest amount of Biblical knowledge with the highest attainments in mental and moral science, and in the great departments of the physical sciences which distinguish this age.

A few thoughts may, however, be suggested as showing, at least, how far the Bible recognizes the propriety of appealing to these principles, and as showing that, thus far, these principles have not come in conflict with the claims of the Bible as a book of revealed truth.

§ 1. *The Bible appeals to the reason of mankind.*

The meaning of this statement is, that the Bible recognizes the doctrine that man is capable of judging of truth, or that there are principles of truth, lying back of its own revelations, to which it appeals, and on which it relies in presenting itself to be received by mankind as a revelation from God; in other words, there *are* eternal truths, not dependent on the mere will of God, to which a true revelation will be conformed. The Bible does not claim to set up its own decision of right and wrong, by ignoring or setting aside all that reason teaches, or by supposing that there is no foundation for judging of what is true or false, right or wrong, in the human soul.

(*a*) This appeal the Bible makes, or presumes to be made, in such passages as the following (Isa. i. 18): "Come, now, and let us reason together, saith the Lord." Here the appeal is made directly to the *reason* of mankind, presuming that there is that in the human mind which will appreciate the force of the arguments which are suggested (see verses 18, 19, 20), and that those arguments will commend themselves to man *as* sound arguments, and as worthy of their attention; that is, it is not assumed in the case that no respect is to be shown to reason; that it is a matter of indifference whether a correct or false principle is stated; that all the force of the appeal depends on the fact that God has made the statement; that it is perfectly arbitrary with him to make a thing reasonable or unreasonable, right or wrong, by a mere statement; or that there is nothing *lying back* of such a statement which is a proper ground of appeal. Just the reverse of all this *is* assumed in the appeal. In fact, God assumes this just as really as we do when we undertake to *reason* with a sinner, and to show him that he is wrong in his conduct. We assume that he is endowed with reason; that he is capable of appreciating the force of an argument; that the fact that a thing is right or wrong in no wise depends, in the case, on our stating it to be so, but that there is something back of our statement, in the mind itself, or in the nature of things, which makes the distinction between right and wrong certain, and which lays the foundation for our appeal.

Thus, also, Paul 'reasoned' with Felix (Acts, xxiv. 25). He did not merely appeal to authority, not even the authority of God. He felt that he was addressing one endowed with reason, and capable of appreciating an argument addressed to reason. He presumed that the commands of God could be so commended to him that he would see their propriety, and be led to yield to their influence and claims. So, in Isaiah, xli. 21, God appeals, by the prophet, to the Hebrew people: "Produce your cause, saith the Lord; bring forth your strong reasons, saith the King of Jacob." This would be unnecessary and improper, unless it were assumed that there is something in man by which he can judge of the reasonableness and propriety of the divine dealings; some ground of judgment in regard even to the acts of God as conformable, or not conformable, to justice and propriety.

And, in general, it may be observed that the Bible is remarkable for its appeals to mankind on the ground of the reasonableness of its commands and its doctrines. Perhaps no book can be found where this kind of appeal is more common, or regarded as more certain. God appeals to man to determine whether idols have the same claim to homage which he has; whether his claims are just; whether his laws are reasonable, easy, proper, equal.

Now, all this supposes that there is *something* lying back of mere command, which is the ground of the appeal; or that man is so made that he can *see* what is just, and right, and good. If this were not so, then all such appeals would be out of place, and would be improper. All the appeal which could be made, if this were not so, would be, that the fact that God wills a thing is all the evidence needed, in any case, that it is right, no matter how repugnant it may be to the reason of mankind.

The same thing is implied in all the statements in the Bible—and they are almost numberless—that God is holy; that he is just; that he is good; that he is true. What can be the meaning of these statements, unless it be assumed that there *is* holiness, justice, goodness, truth, in the nature of things, or apart from the mere will of God? If all the holiness, justice, goodness, and truth which there is in the universe, is founded on the mere will of God, arbitrarily *making* a thing holy, just, good, and true, then such an appeal could have no force. It is, in fact, no more than saying that God *is*, and what he chooses to make holy is holy; what he wills to make just is just; what he wills to make good is good; what he wills to make true is true. On that supposition, there is no standard of appeal in the case, and such an appeal would be, in fact, mere illusion. I affirm that my conduct is right. According to this supposition, all that I mean by the affirmation is that my conduct is what I please, and that I choose to *make* my conduct the standard of right. I affirm of another that his conduct is *just;* when asked to explain myself, I answer that all that I mean is that his conduct is what he pleases it should be, and that, by his own will, he makes any actions which he performs, right or wrong, and that his conduct, in this particular case, is right, because he has chosen to affix the word *just* to one part of his conduct, and *good* to another, and *holy* to another. There is no standard back of this. There is no general judgment of mankind to which an appeal lies. There is nothing in the nature of things which makes one act more true, or holy, or just, or good than another, or which makes it proper to affix these terms to it: for all depends on the mere will of him who performs the act. All that could be meant by such an appeal, in regard to God, would be, that he has done what he has chosen to do, and that the fact that he has done it is a sufficient reason why it is right. He has not done it *because* it is right, but it is right because he has done it; that is, all that there is in man which pronounces anything right or wrong; all that he has been made, by the laws of his nature, to regard as right or wrong; and all the appeals to him based on this, in respect to the character of God, is to go for naught: for it is all based on the false assumption that there *is* such a thing as right and wrong in the nature of things. Such was not the faith of Abraham. "Shall not the Judge of all the earth DO RIGHT?" was *his* language, when he stood before God, and plead for guilty Sodom. Gen. xviii. 25. *He* felt, evidently, that there is such a thing as "right," in itself considered. He felt assured that the Judge of all the earth *would* do right—that which is right in itself considered, and apart from mere will. He felt that what God might be about to do (destroying the righteous with the wicked) would expose him to the charge of doing that which men would regard as wrong, and he made this the basis of his argument with his Maker, not that he would do a thing, and *make* it right by his doing it, or make that the only ground of vindicating his character, but that he would do that which was right and proper in itself—which would commend itself to the mind of Abraham, and to the minds of men at large, as *right.*

An expression which will illustrate this thought occurs, also, in Jeremiah xiv. 21: "Do not abhor us, for thy name's sake; *do not disgrace the throne of thy glory;* remember, break not thy covenant with us." In this language it is implied that there is a course which would be becoming for God, or which would be appropriate to his character; and that there is a course which would be unbecoming, dishonorable, and disgraceful to his character. In other words, there must be something in man which makes him capable of judging what it would be proper for God to do, or something lying back of mere will, and different from the mere fact that God does it, which would make it right. If the mere fact that God does or wills a thing always makes it right, then there would be no ground for such

6

a judgment, and no reason for such a plea as that made by Jeremiah, since, in that case, the mere fact that God does it would preserve his character and doings from "disgrace."

Perhaps no book has ever been written which so often and so constantly appeals to the *reason* of mankind as the Bible. It all along assumes that there is such a thing as right and wrong in themselves considered, and that the laws and requirements of God are such as *are* in themselves right; not that they are *made* right by sovereign will.

(*b*) Men argue in the same way about the Bible. The friends of the Bible assume that this is a correct mode of reasoning, and they probably make many more appeals of this kind than any other class of men.

1. All the evidences of the truth of divine revelation are based on this idea. The appeal from miracles, from prophecy, and from the doctrines of the Bible, are appeals to the *reason* of men, who, in such arguments, are presumed to be capable of judging in the case whether the Bible *is* such a revelation as it becomes God to make, or is *reasonable* in its claims on mankind. If there was no such power of judging, then such appeals would have no force; and if the arguments addressed to men in favor of the Bible cannot be made to commend themselves to reason, even the advocates and defenders of the Bible assume that it cannot be received by the world. There are none of those defenders who would attempt to urge men to receive a book whose principles and commands were admitted by themselves to be *unreasonable*, nor could they hope or expect to be able to convince men that such a book *ought* to be received by mankind. They may attempt to show,

and they may do it successfully, that many of the statements in revelation are *above* the reason of mankind, and that the statements of a revelation from God may be expected to bear this character, and that this fact should be no barrier to the reception of the book as a revelation; but no one would maintain that the statements of a revelation from God are to be expected to be *contradictory* to reason, and should not on that account be rejected. It is always assumed in all the arguments in favor of a revelation, that if the statements in the book are contradictory to reason, or are not consistent with the best exercise of reason, the book cannot be received; for it is assumed that God is the author of reason, and that all the statements which He makes must be consistent with the proper exercise of the faculties with which He has endowed mankind.

2. Men *preach* in this way. They expect to commend the doctrines which they preach to the reason of their hearers, or, at least, to show that they are not contradictory to the proper laws of reason; and if they cannot do this, they have no hope of being successful. It is their hope and their belief that they may be able so to present the doctrines which they preach, that they shall appear to their hearers to be *reasonable* doctrines, or, at least, if the positive reasonableness of the doctrines cannot be made apparent, that they shall not be *unreasonable*, or contrary to reason; and in proportion as they can do this, they entertain the hope that their doctrines will be received by mankind. They would entertain no hope if the doctrines which they preach were palpably contrary to reason, or if the arguments by which they were sustained were at variance with all the rules of logic; and though for the *authority* of

those doctrines, and for their binding obligation, they depend on the will of God; and though they promulgate doctrines which are above reason, or which reason could never have discovered, yet they could have no hope of success if their doctrines were a violation of the plain dictates of reason, nor could they entertain such a hope if they were unable to show that it is *reasonable* that man should obey the will of God. All this supposes that there is something besides mere *will*—even the will of God—in the case; that there is something back of that will which makes that will right and proper. If it were not so, then all reasoning on the doctrines of religion would be vain and useless; then it would be of no consequence to be able to show that it is reasonable to obey the will of God; then it would be a matter of indifference what doctrines were inculcated for human belief, provided it were shown us that they were the exponents of the will of God; then it would be difficult to see why man was endowed with reason, or why he was so made that there would be danger that he would regard this as of importance in religion. Then, too, it would be difficult to account for the fact that God so made the mind of man that he naturally employs the aid of reason in judging of the subject of religion—since, if it were true that reason has nothing to do with religion, or if it were improper to make any appeal to it, it would seem that God had so made the mind as to lead necessarily to a perpetual mistake on the subject, by having so endowed man that he naturally supposes that this *is* a competent tribunal before which to bring the doctrines of religion. Then, also, it would follow that they who should show the least deference to reason in their preaching, or whose doctrines were most difficult to be reconciled to reason—that is, most *absurd*—would be likely to be most successful in their preaching; a maxim which, however it may seem to be acted on by many in their preaching, would not be likely to be one that would be openly avowed. Then, also, it would follow that the labor of Butler in the "Analogy," was a useless, if not a pernicious labor, for the great object of that immortal work is to show that revealed religion is reasonable, since it conforms in its great principles to the constitution and course of nature; and then, too, it would seem that nothing was gained by so endowing President Edwards with the power of ratiocination that in this respect he should, by common consent, be placed at the head of the race, and by inclining him to exert those great powers in showing that the doctrines of revealed religion are conformable to the highest deductions of reason, since the whole work which he performed proceeded on the supposition that reason is, in some way, a proper tribunal before which to bring the doctrines of revealed religion. All the reasoning in Butler and Edwards proceeds on the supposition that there is a standard of judging distinct from mere *will*, and that the doctrines of revelation commend themselves to men because the will of God *is* conformable to such a standard, and may be judged of by reason.

3. The same thing follows from all the attempts which are made to vindicate the character of God. If his will is not only the ultimate, but the only standard, or, in other words, if it is his will only which makes anything right or wrong, then it would seem to be impossible, in any proper sense, to vindicate his character, and as needless as it is impossible, since all that would

be necessary or proper in the case would be simply to show what he *is*, what he *wills*, and what he *does*. For, what is it to *vindicate* a character? It is: "to defend, to justify, to support or maintain *as true or correct, against denial, censure, or objection*."—*Webster*. That is, it is to show that what is thus vindicated or defended is worthy of confidence as judged by some standard of integrity. When we vindicate the character of a lawgiver, it is with reference to the constitution under which he acts, and the proprieties of his station; when we vindicate the character of a magistrate, it is with reference to the law by which he is appointed, and the integrity demanded in his office; when we vindicate the character of a neighbor, it is with reference to some rule of morality or propriety in the intercourse of man with man. We affirm, in such cases, of a man, that he is upright, moral, pure, just, chaste, benevolent, impartial; that is, we have an *idea* of what it is to be upright, moral, pure, just, chaste, benevolent, impartial, and we judge of him with reference to the conformity of his conduct to that standard. What is meant when it is said that God is *holy?* Do men intend to say that God, by his mere will, determines a thing *to be* holy, and then simply that his conduct is conformable to his own will? Can this truism be all that is meant when men maintain respecting God, or when God affirms of himself, that he is *holy?* What is meant where it is affirmed that he is *righteous*, or that his conduct is *just?* Do men mean that he, by a mere determination of will, *makes* a thing to be righteous or just, and then that his own conduct is conformable to what he has been pleased to *make righteous or just?* Was this all that Abraham meant when he said: "Shall not the Judge of all the earth do *right?*"

And in vindicating the higher doctrines of Christianity—the doctrine of the Trinity, the incarnation, the atonement, and the Scripture statement in regard to future retribution—do not the friends and advocates of those doctrines endeavor to prove that such truths do not *violate* any of the principles of sound reason? While they cheerfully admit that they are above reason, in the sense that reason could not have discovered them, and that the reason of man is not competent now, if it will ever be, fully to comprehend them, is it ever conceded that they are contrary to sound reason? Do not the advocates of those doctrines steadfastly maintain that if the understanding of man was sufficiently comprehensive to embrace them in the fulness of their meaning, that they would be said to be in entire accordance with the principles of sound reason? Could they hope or expect that they would secure the assent of mankind, if, while they are stated to be *above* reason, they should also be admitted to be *contrary* to reason? And, in particular, in regard to the doctrine of future punishment—the eternal sufferings of any portion of the creatures of God—the most difficult and incomprehensible of all the doctrines of the Bible, do not the advocates of that doctrine always maintain that there are *reasons* for the eternal punishment of the wicked which will be satisfactory to the universe when they are understood; that if those reasons could be seen now the mind would acquiesce in them; and that it will be seen hereafter that, fearful as that doctrine is, the character of God, even in inflicting the punishment, is worthy of universal confidence and love? We have, in fact, the following statement in the Bible itself, in regard to the effect on holy beings of the inflictions of God's just judgment on the wicked: "I heard a great voice of much people in heaven, saying, Alleluia! salvation, and glory, and honor, and power unto the Lord our God; for true and righteous are his judgments. And again they said, Alleluia. And her smoke rose up forever and ever."—Rev. xix. 1–3. And in all these attempts to vindicate these doctrines; to vindicate the character of God in view of these doctrines; to show that these doctrines are conformable to reason, and that the character of God is holy, just, and righteous, is it not implied that there is something *back* of mere *will* that is an element in judging; that there *is* some standard of what is reasonable and right, by which God admits that even his own character is to be judged? Has he not made us so that it is necessary that the doctrines which he reveals, as well as his own conduct and character, shall be seen to be conformable to that standard before we can perceive that he is worthy of confidence and love? Has he not so made us that we could not honor him if it was seen by us that his character and dealings were in violation of those principles which he has made to be the standard by which our own minds determine what is right? When God appeals to us, and when men attempt to vindicate his character, is the ground of the appeal and of the vindication, the mere fact that God has done what he has done, and that, therefore, it is right, or that all that is right in his act is in his will; or is it that there is such a thing as right in itself, and that we have been so made, after his own image, that we can see and appreciate what is right when it is fairly submitted to our understanding? If this is not so, what do men mean when they attempt to *vindicate* the character of God? Certain it is that the statements in the Bible are founded on the supposition that the laws of God, and the dealings of God, can be so presented to the minds of men that they will be seen to be *right;* that they will be seen to be not mere expressions of will, but the expressions of eternal justice, goodness, and truth. And certain it is that whatever men may maintain in regard to the question whether there is such a thing as right and wrong in the nature of things with which the divine dealings will be found to accord, and by which he judges of his own conduct, and expects to be judged by others, they always proceed on this supposition in all their attempts to vindicate God.

4. It is worthy of serious inquiry what the character of God *is* if this is not so. Let it be assumed that there is no such thing as right and wrong in themselves, or in the nature of things; that all this is determined by mere will; that that is right which God has made right, and that wrong which he has made wrong, and that the one is right and the other wrong only because he has made them so, and then what, on this supposition, is the character of God, and what is the claim which he has to the homage, the confidence, and the love of the universe which he has made?

The following consequences would seem to follow inevitably from such an assumption:—

(*a*) That of such a character we know not whether it is good or evil; or rather it is, in fact, neither, since all that is to determine whether it is good or evil is in his own will. We cannot apply the terms good or evil to such a character, for the terms, in such a case, convey no idea. We can predicate *power* of such a being; we can predicate of him sagacity, wisdom, skill; we can also predicate benevolence, for the tendency of his acts may be to promote happiness; but how can we predicate *right* or *wrong* of such a being; or how can we say that his benevolence is a virtue, unless it be assumed that there *is* such a thing as right, and that benevolence is a virtue because it is right?

(*b*) A malignant being might be all that would be implied in the idea under consideration. If clothed with absolute authority and power, he might determine, by an act of will, that his own deeds were right; that his will was the standard, and that the good or evil of all acts was to be determined by that will. If, for example, the laws of such a being were just the reverse of what the laws of God are, it is impossible to see, on the supposition now under consideration, how they could be disapproved of by mankind, or how they could be regarded as wrong, since, by the supposition, all that there is of moral character in such acts and laws is determined solely by the will of the being himself.

(*c*) In such a case, also, there would be a jar or discrepancy between our nature as God has made us, and the conclusion which we should be compelled to come to respecting himself. There can be no doubt that we have been so made that we are under a necessity of believing that there is such a thing as right and wrong, or that the human mind, when it acts freely, comes to this conclusion; and there can be as little doubt that we have been so made as to apply this mode of judging to the acts of our Maker as well as our own; in other words, to judge him and his doings by this as a standard. The considerations which have been suggested above seem to be conclusive on this point. If this be true, then it would follow that he has so formed us that there is a jar or discrepancy which he has himself made between what is true and what, by the laws of our nature, we are so constituted as to regard as true; that is, he has so made us that we apply this rule of judging to all things, even to his own character and acts, while, in fact, there *is* no such thing in existence. There *is* no right and wrong such as we assume in our judgments, and the supposition that there is is a mere fallacy. *Why* God should have made us so, would then be a grave matter of consideration. *Why* he has so constituted us that we should pass through this world at least under a constant illusion—a practical falsehood—would be a problem that would perplex us more than any of the existing facts in the other supposition. What confidence we should have in such a being, or why we should exercise any confidence in him, would be questions which, indeed, it might be easy to solve, but the solution would cast a darker shadow over the universe than has been thrown over it by what we are now constrained to regard as sin, as evil in itself and evil in its tendency. If there is anything on which the human mind is perfectly settled and firm in its conclusions, it is that the interpretations which it is designed by our constitution that we shall put on the acts of our Maker, are such as are in accordance with truth, or that they give a fair exposition of his character. What he meant should be regarded as true is not falsehood; what he has made us to regard as right cannot be wrong.

(*d*) Further; on the supposition now under consideration, we should not know what we worshipped. We approach God now, taught by all the constitutional laws of our being, as a God of holiness, justice, truth, goodness, mercy, meaning by those terms all that they naturally and properly convey. We suppose that they do mean something; that they mean all that can be understood to be implied in them. In the most absolute and unconditional sense, we feel that God *is* holy, just, true, good, and merciful. Our feelings in our worship are not distracted and divided by such questions as these: whether these terms mean anything; whether all that there is in the case is not the mere result of will; whether we have not mistaken the proper interpretation to be put on the acts of our Maker; and whether all that we have heretofore regarded as reality is not, in fact, mere illusion; that all this is the appointment of mere *will*—a will which might have made just the reverse of these things to be proper and right if God had chosen that it should be so.

Who could honor such a God? How true in such a case, in reference to all those who now desire to worship the true God, would be the declaration of the Saviour in regard to the Samaritans: "Ye worship ye know not what."—John iv. 22.

But the God of the Bible is *not* such a God. He is a God who *is* holy, and just, and true, and good, and merciful; a God, the Judge of all the earth, who does "right" (Gen. viii. 25); "a God of truth and without iniquity, JUST AND RIGHT IS HE."—Deut. xxxii. 4.

§ 2. *The Bible appeals to the conscience or moral sense of mankind.*

The meaning of this proposition is, that the Bible presumes that there is a conscience in man, or that he is endowed with a capability of judging of right and wrong. It is further meant that this power of judging, so far, at least, as to be a proper ground of appeal, lies back of the direct teachings of revelation, and that whatever a revelation may do in enlarging or correcting the power of judging, it presumes that it, in fact, exists in the mind of man. And still further, the meaning of the proposition is, that the Bible presumes that its own distinct and peculiar revelations on the subjects of right and wrong will so commend themselves to mankind, that they will *see* that its commands are right; so that they may be made to feel the consciousness of guilt for not obeying those commands, and so that they will approve of them as founded on eternal principles of justice.

In illustration and proof of this proposition, I submit the following remarks:—

(1) The Bible expressly makes this appeal, and relies on it as one of the foundations of its hopes of success in diffusing its truths. Thus the Apostle Paul says (2 Cor. iv. 1, 2): "Therefore, seeing we have this ministry, as we have received mercy, we faint not: but have renounced the hidden things of dishonesty, not walking in craftiness, nor handling the word of God deceitfully; but by manifestation of the truth commending ourselves to every man's conscience in the sight of God." Here it is assumed that there are such things as dishonesty and deceit—things that are "dark" in their nature or "hidden"—things that will

not bear the light of day, and it was with the apostle a fixed purpose to renounce all such methods of influencing men—never assuming that it is the province of revelation to make that appear right which men, in these respects, regard as wrong, or to assume that men have no correct judgment of what is right and wrong. It is assumed further that men have a "conscience," even when they have no revelation, and that that conscience is competent to pronounce a judgment on the doctrines of revelation. It is assumed further that the true way of meeting the demands of such a conscience is to be found in "the manifestation of the *truth*." And it is further assumed that "truth"—the revealed truth of God—even the highest and the holiest of the truths which He has revealed—can be so presented to the minds of men as to secure the approbation of conscience; that is, so that there shall be an entire correspondence between the truths so presented and the decisions of conscience as to what is right. It is obvious that no such appeal could be made on the supposition that there is no such thing as right and wrong in themselves considered, or if men have no power of any kind of judging of what is right or wrong. If right and wrong are determined by an arbitrary decree, then it is clear that it would be utterly in vain, and wholly improper, to make such an appeal as that referred to by the apostle in the passage before us; and it is also clear that, on that supposition, the style and drift of his preaching would have been quite different from that implied in this passage. The substance of his preaching, in such a case, must have been that God may determine, without any reference to the nature of things, or the nature of men, what is right, and that he may require that that shall be received as right, however it may *appear* to man. In such a case the last thing that would be done would be to make an appeal to the moral sense of mankind.

A similar passage occurs in 2 Cor. vi. 4. "*In all things approving* [marg. *commending*] *ourselves as the ministers of God:*" that is, by showing to mankind that we pursue such a course of life as they must *see* to be in accordance with what the ministers of religion should be —to wit, "by pureness, by knowledge, by long suffering, by kindness, by the Holy Ghost, by love unfeigned, by the word of truth, by the power of God, by the armor of righteousness:" vs. 6, 7. Here it is assumed that there is a course of life which men must perceive to be *proper* for the ministers of religion; a course of life in reference to which they form a judgment from the promptings of their nature; a course which is fit in itself, and which it is reasonable for men to expect and demand in those who claim to be ministers of a revealed religion.

A passage of similar import occurs in Romans v. 8: "God commendeth his love toward us, in that, while we were yet sinners, Christ died for us." That is, he appeals to us in proof that that was a proper expression of love; that it was such an act as love would suggest, and such as ought to meet the approval of mankind. It is assumed here that men are endowed with the faculty of judging what is proper and right as an expression of love, and that all that is demanded in such an expression was found in the act of God in giving His Son to die for men when they were yet sinners. There was that which, in the nature of things, was demanded as the proper expression of love, and all this was found in the work of redemption.

A statement similar to those just made, and confirming the inferences drawn from them, occurs in Romans ii. 14, 15: "When the Gentiles, which have not the law, do by nature the things contained in the law, these having not the law, are a law unto themselves: which show the work of the law written in their hearts, their conscience also bearing witness, and their thoughts the meanwhile accusing, or else excusing one another." In this passage, all that has been affirmed in the previous pages on the point now under consideration, is implied. It is supposed that men have a conscience, or that they are endowed with a power of judging of right and wrong; it is assumed that there is such a thing as right and wrong independently of the revealed will of God; it is assumed that their conviction of what is right has to them with propriety the force of law; it is assumed that these things accord with the revealed law of God; and, of course, it is assumed that the revealed law or will of God will commend itself to their consciences, or will be such as they will approve. It is supposed, moreover, that this law is so uniform in its operations among the Gentiles, even amidst all the errors which prevail, as to show that it has its foundation in the nature of man, and is not dependent on local laws and local legislation. In other words, there is something in man everywhere which responds to the notions of right and wrong, and which, as it approves of right as far as it is known, it is to be presumed will approve of right when its higher claims are disclosed by revelation. The sadness of the condition in the heathen world was not that they did not understand the distinction between right and wrong, or that they did not know what was right, but it was that they did that which they knew to be wrong, or which their own consciences condemned.

A similar passage also occurs in Phil. iv. 8. "Whatsoever things are true, whatsoever things are honest, whatsoever things are just, whatsoever things are pure, whatsoever things are lovely, whatsoever things are of good report; if there be any virtue, and if there be any praise, think on these things." Here it is assumed that there *are* things which in their own nature are true, honest, just, pure, lovely, and of good report; that there *is* such a thing as virtue, and that there are things which are deserving of praise or commendation, and these are presented as objects of pursuit by all true Christians. There is a standard of right and wrong. It is not a mere arbitrary standard made by revelation. There are things which men universally approve as true, and just, and pure, and lovely; and these, whatever other virtues Christians may have, should be found in their own character, as commending their religion to their fellow men.

(2) The point here stated is assumed by all who attempt to defend the Bible. They endeavor to show that the precepts of the Bible are such as are adapted to meet the approbation of conscience, and that they ought to meet that approbation. They endeavor to prove that, while, in very many respects, the precepts of the Bible are in advance of the disclosures of duty made by conscience, up to the point where disclosures are made, conscience and the Bible harmonize, and that the higher disclosures are but carrying out the same principles. They endeavor to demonstrate

that the precepts of the Bible meet the demands of conscience, and that they are such as, being obeyed, would produce in the highest degree the happiness of men.

This argument will be found in all the works which are designed to enforce the laws of the Bible, and in all the books on morality which are founded on the authority of that book. A man would not seriously set himself to write a book in defence of the Bible if, in order to his undertaking, it was necessary to admit that the precepts of the Bible are a violation of the convictions of men in regard to natural justice, truth, probity, chastity, honor, and honesty, and if, in order to his argument, it was necessary to show that the views usually entertained on those subjects are false, and are to be set aside in the purest system of morals.

The Bible makes its way among men, and sustains its hold on society as it advances in intelligence and morality, *because* its precepts commend themselves to the moral sense of mankind. It is not so much by abstract argument; it is not so much because men always have before their minds distinctly the recollection of the argument from miracles and prophecy; it is because men see the truth and beauty of the moral precepts of the book itself, and because those precepts commend themselves to them *as* true, and useful, and good.

(3) As a matter of fact, the precepts of the Bible *do* thus commend themselves to mankind. The grounds of objection to the Bible have never, to any extent, been drawn from its moral precepts. In fact, those precepts have gone into the legislation, and the business arrangements of the world, and are admitted by

the great mass of mankind to be the true foundation of morals. The laws in the Decalogue; the command to love God and our neighbor; the injunctions requiring us to be meek, gentle, pure, benevolent, chaste, forgiving; the rules laid down in the Bible relating to parents and children, husbands and wives, masters and servants; the precepts respecting the proper treatment of the poor and needy, the down-trodden and the oppressed, the widow and the fatherless, the stranger and the prisoner, are such as all men must and do approve. They commend themselves to them as in entire accordance with those great principles of morality which have been engraven on their nature, and as being adapted to promote the highest interests of society. Every man must see and admit that if those directions were obeyed by all men, the world would at once put on a new aspect, and that peace and happiness would be diffused over the globe.

It is true that not a few of these rules when they were given were in advance of the prevailing opinions and customs of the world. It is true, for example, that the commands in the New Testament forbidding revenge, and enjoining the forgiveness of injuries, were at first in conflict with many opinions which then prevailed, and many of the arrangements in society, for many of the customs of the world had been formed on the supposition that revenge *should* be taken, and that an enemy should *not* be forgiven; but it is true also that society, in its progress, has *come up* to these precepts, and that the customs of the world are more and more shaping themselves to the doctrines of the New Testament on these points. Society will yet adjust itself into entire conformity with those rules.

It is, however, to be admitted that some of the commands of the Old Testament have been made a ground of objection to the Bible, as being irreconcilable with the injunctions of the New Testament, or with just principles of morality. The most prominent instances of this nature would probably be the command to Abraham to offer his son in sacrifice; and the command to the invading Hebrews to exterminate the inhabitants of the land of Canaan. It may be proper to consider how far these should be regarded as constituting an objection to the Bible.

Mr. Newman, in his work on the "Soul," affirms that in many cases the Bible sanctions, and even enjoins, things which shock his moral sense as flagrantly immoral, and that he *must*, therefore, reject the Bible. He, in different places of his work, gives three instances: the assassination of Sisera, by the wife of Heber; the command to Abraham to sacrifice his son; and the extermination of the Canaanites. The first of these certainly may be laid out of the account, as there is no evidence that God *authorized* the assassination, and there is as little evidence that he has expressed any approbation of it as there is that he did of the murder of Uriah by David. The second and third instances deserve a more formal notice, as it is presumed, from the fact that these cases are selected, that they are the most difficult, and as the principles of explanation to be applied to them would eventually meet *all* the instances in the Bible.

In reference to the latter of these two—the command to exterminate the inhabitants of Canaan—it may be remarked (*a*) that the command is expressly placed on the ground of the amazing depravity of those nations, as if the cup of their iniquity was full; (*b*) that what actually occurred was attended with no *more* horror or suffering than what *actually* occurs on the earth as a consequence of storms, earthquakes, plagues, and famines; (*c*) that it is no real ground of objection to the character of God that he gives command to storms, and plagues, and famines, to sweep away, amidst scenes of vast suffering, men, women, and children by thousands and tens of thousands; (*d*) that it is difficult to see why a command might not with the same propriety be given to *men* to execute such a work of justice; (*e*) that it is no reflection on the character of an executive of a government that he issues a warrant to a sheriff for the execution of a man convicted of crime, or for the sheriff to carry the command into execution; (*f*) that the commands in question were in no sense a departure from what was understood at the time to be proper in war; and (*g*) that those commands were not given as a general rule in the treatment of other nations, but as a special rule in reference to those who had become incorrigibly wicked, and whom God had resolved to remove from the earth. It is difficult to see how that command can be objected to, unless the objection shall be made to lie also against God's right to dispose of wicked nations, and against what he actually does in sweeping off by other than human agents vast multitudes of people—people of either sex, the aged, the helpless, and the young, in the horrors of conflagration, shipwreck, pestilence, and famine. If a man will make the trial, he will see that it may be as easy to vindicate the character of God in respect to the one as in respect to the other: and admitting that that was a special case, and not designed for the general direction of mankind, it will be easy to see that the precepts of the Bible in regard to peace, and the forgiveness of enemies, and the treatment of the aged, the feeble, and the helpless, are such as commend themselves to all men as in accordance with every sentiment of humanity and justice.

In one word, the case must be considered *just as it is represented in the Bible.* It is not a general command to make war; it is not an injunction to inflict cruelty on enemies in general; it is not a rule which can be alleged by one who is disposed to invade an unoffending people; *it is a command to inflict punishment on a specified people of eminent wickedness, and* ON ACCOUNT *of their wickedness, and* FOR NO OTHER CAUSE: a command *as* specific as a death-warrant, addressed to a sheriff, in respect to a man convicted of murder, or as specific as we may suppose his command is to earthquakes, to storms, to the pestilence, to sweep off the aged, and the helpless, and the harmless, in horrors more deep, more dreadful, and more prolonged than those of war. For anything that appears to the contrary, a sheriff might, with just as much propriety, urge the fact that a death-warrant has been directed to him against a convicted murderer, as authority for inflicting indiscriminate vengeance on all classes of men, as any one now could urge the command to exterminate the Canaanites as justifying offensive war; or an objector might argue, with just as much propriety, that the laws of the United States, or of England, are such as to "shock the moral sense of mankind," because they direct such a death-warrant to an executioner, as to draw a similar inference in regard to the character of God from the command to exterminate the Canaanites.

In reference to this command, the following remarks by the author of the *Eclipse of Faith* (pp. 149, 150, 151, 152, 153), seem to me to be so forcible that I copy them. They show that the objection should have a higher range than it has when levelled against the Bible; that it is, in fact, an objection against the actual government of the world, and, therefore, is not one with which the defender of the Bible has any *peculiar* concern.

"Now, whether the Bible represents God, or not, in all these cases, as sanctioning the things in question, I shall not be at the pains to inquire, because I am willing to take it for granted that Mr. Newman's representation is perfectly correct. I only think that he ought, in consistency, to have gone a little further. Let him defend, as in perfect harmony with his 'intuitions' of right and wrong, the undeniably similar instances which occur in the administration of the universe; or, if it be found impossible to solve those difficulties, let him acknowledge either that our supposed essential 'intuitions' of moral rectitude are not to be trusted, as applicable to the Supreme Being, and that, therefore, the argument *from* them against the Bible is inconclusive; or, that no such being exists; or, lastly, that He has conferred upon man an intuitive conception of moral equity and rectitude—of the just and the unjust—in most edifying contradiction to his own character and proceedings!

"Here Fellowes broke in:—

"'If, indeed, there *be* any such instances; but I think Mr. Newman would reply that they will be sought for in vain in the 'world,' however plentiful, as I admit they are, in the Bible.'

"'I know not whether he would deny them or not,' said Harrington; 'but they are found in great abundance in the world, notwithstanding, and this is my difficulty. If Mr. Newman were the creator of the universe, no question, none of these contradictions between 'intuitions' within and stubborn 'facts' without, would be found. He has created a God after his own mind; if he could but have created a universe also after his own mind, we should, doubtless, have been relieved from all our perplexities. But, unhappily, we find in it, as I imagine, the very things which so startle Mr. Newman in the Scriptural representations of the divine character and proceedings. Is he not, like all other infidels, peculiarly scandalized that God should have *enjoined* the extermination of the Canaanites? and yet does not God *do* still more startling things every day of our lives, and which appear *less* startling only because we are familiar with them—at least, if we believe that the elements, pestilence, famine, in a word, destruction in all its forms, really fulfil *his* bidding? Is there any difference in the world between the cases, except that the terrible phenomena which we find it impossible to account for are on an infinitely larger scale, and in duration as ancient as the world—that they have, in fact, been going on for thousands of weary years, and, for aught you or I can tell, and as Mr. Newman seems to think probable, for millions of years? Does not a pestilence or a famine send thousands of the guilty and the innocent alike—nay, thousands of those who know not their right hand from their left—to one common destruction? Does not God (if you suppose it his doing) swallow up whole cities by earthquake, or overwhelm them with volcanic fires? I say is there any difference between the cases, except that the victims are very rarely so wicked as the Canaanites are said to have been, and that God in the one case *himself* does the very things which he commissions men to do in the other? Now, if the *thing* be wrong, I, for one, shall never think it less wrong to do it one's self than to do it by proxy.'

"'But,' said Fellowes, rather warmly, for he felt rather restive at this part of Harrington's discourse, 'it is absurd to compare such *sovereign* acts of inexplicable will on the part of God with his *command* to a being so constituted as man to perform them.'

"'Absurd be it,' said Harrington, 'only be so kind as to *show* it to be so, instead of saying so. I maintain that the one class of facts are just as 'inexplicable,' as you call it, as the other, and only appear otherwise because, in the one case, we daily see them, have become accustomed to them, and what is more than all, *cannot deny* them, which last we can so promptly do in the other case, for Moses is not here to contradict us. But I rather think that a being constituted morally and intellectually like us, who had never known *any* but a world of happiness, would just as promptly deny that God could ever perform such feats as are daily performed in *this* world! I repeat that, if, for some reasons ('inexplicable,' I grant you), God does not mind *doing* such things, he is not likely to hesitate to *enjoin* them, for reasons *perhaps* equally inexplicable. I say *perhaps*, for, as I compare such an event as the earthquake in Lisbon, or the plague in London, with the extermination of the Canaanites, I solemnly assure you that I find a greater difficulty, as far as my 'intuitions' go, in supposing the former event to have been effected by a *divine* agency than the latter. If we take the Scripture history, we must at least allow that the race thus doomed had long tried the patience of Heaven by their flagrant impiety and unnatural vices; that they had become a centre and a source (as we sometimes see collections of men to be) of moral pestilence, in the vicinage of which it was unsafe for men to dwell; that, as the Scriptures say (whether truly or falsely I do not inquire), they had 'filled up the measure of their iniquities.' Let this be supposed as fictitious as you please, still the whole proceeding is *represented* as a solemn judicial one; and, supposing the events to have occurred just as they are narrated, it positively seems to me much less difficult to suppose them to harmonize with the character of a just and even beneficent being, than those wholesale butcheries which have desolated the world, in every hour of its long history, without any discrimination whatever of innocence or guilt; which, if they have inflicted unspeakable miseries on the immediate victims, have produced probably as much, or more, in the agony of the myriad myriads of hearts which have bled or broken in unavailing sorrow over the sufferings they could not relieve. Such things (I speak now only of what man has not, in any sense, inflicted) are, in your view, as undeniably the work of God as is the extermination of the Canaanites, according to the Bible. Why, if God does not mind *doing* such things, are we to suppose that he minds, on some occasions, ordering them to be *done*, unless we suppose that man (delicate creature) has more refined intuitions of right and wrong, and knows better what they are, than God himself? Now, Mr. Newman and you affirm that, to suppose God should have *enjoined* the destruction of the Canaanites, is a contradiction of our moral intuitions, and that, for this and similar reasons, you cannot believe the Bible to be the *word* of God. I answer that the things I have mentioned are in still more glaring contradiction to such 'intuitions,' than which none appears to me more clear than this: that the morally innocent ought not to suffer; and I therefore doubt whether the above phenomena are the work of God. I must refuse, on the very same principle on which Mr. Newman disallows the Bible to be a true revelation of such a Being, to allow this universe to be so. In equally glaring inconsistency is the entire administration of this lower world with what appears to me a first principle of moral rectitude, namely, that he who suffers a wrong to be inflicted on another, when *he can prevent* it, is responsible for the wrong itself. The whole world is full of such instances.' "

The command addressed to Abraham to offer his son as a sacrifice, is a difficulty of a similar character, but of a higher kind. It would be said that the command is a violation of all the instinctive feelings of our nature; that it enjoins the perpetration of what has everywhere been regarded as a crime of the highest character, and one most rarely committed even by depraved men—the murder of a son; that we are even shocked at what has been regarded as the rigid Roman virtue of Brutus who presided on the trial of his son, and condemned him to death; that there *could be* no sufficient evidence furnished to Abraham that a command to do this came from God; that so strong is the instinctive feeling of love to a child implanted in our very nature, and so universal is that feeling, that Abraham should have at once rejected any supposed command to imbrue his own hand in the blood of his son as illusory; and that men ought not to receive a book as a revelation from God, in which there occurs a command so shocking to the purest feelings, the holiest instincts, and the best "intentions" of mankind.

As this case is undoubtedly the strongest of the kind that could be referred to, and as it involves all the difficulty that can be found in any case, it may be proper to notice it a little more particularly.

1. The first remark to be made is, that it is important to ascertain exactly what *the case was*, and the objections should be considered in view *of the exact case*, for an objector has no right to go beyond that, or to include in his objection anything which does not properly belong to the case. The *facts*, then, are these:—

First. The command given to Abraham was a *special*, not a *general* command. It was addressed to him, and to no other. It related to that time, and to that son, and to no other time and to no other son. It was not a general rule in regard to his authority over his children; it would not have justified him in a similar treatment of another son; nor would it justify another parent in the same treatment of a child. It was not in itself so general, nor did it involve any principle so general, that it could be a guide in any other case, and it does not, therefore, stand on the same level as the general command inwrought into our nature, and confirmed by revelation, to love our children, to protect them, to provide for them.

Second. The command related to his offering him as a sacrifice to God, on the principle of devoting to him that which was most valued and most valuable. "Take now thy son, thine only son Isaac, whom thou lovest, and get thee into the land of Moriah, and offer him there for a burnt-offering upon one of the mountains which I will tell thee of."—Gen. xxii. 3. Whatever objection, therefore, may lie against the narrative, it can be only in this point of view: not whether a command authorizing a parent to take the life of a son for *any* object would be proper, but whether it would be proper for God to command a man to offer his son, in a specified case, as a burnt-offering. Great as may be the difficulties in regard to this, yet this is *the* difficulty, and the *only* difficulty, and the subject should not be encumbered with any additional embarrassment. This is at least a simple and a tangible question, whether it would be right for God to command a father to devote his own son as a sacrifice.

Third. It is plain that Abraham supposed that Isaac would be raised to life again. This *might* be inferred from the very narrative in Genesis; for there was an express promise made before this that Isaac should be the ancestor of a numerous posterity, and that through him all the nations of the earth should be blessed. Thus, in Gen. xxi. 12, God is represented as saying to Abraham, "In Isaac shall thy seed be called." Comp. Gen. xvii. 5, 6, 7, 8, 9. As this promise was positive, Abraham must have believed that no command from God could conflict with it, and he must have inferred, therefore, that even if Isaac should be offered in sacrifice, God would raise him up again from the dead. But this, which would seem to be so plain as a matter of inference, is expressly stated by an apostle to have been the fact. "By faith Abraham, when he was tried, offered up Isaac; and he that had received the promises offered up his only-begotten son, of whom it was said, that in Isaac shall thy seed be called: Accounting that God was able to raise him up, even from the dead."—Heb. xi. 17–19.

Fourth. It is manifest that it was never intended that Abraham should be allowed to proceed so far in the transaction as actually to imbrue his hands in the blood of his son. This is apparent not only from the result, or from the fact that he was checked when about to slay him, but from the statement which accompanies the account of the transaction: "Lay not thine hand upon the lad, neither do thou anything unto him, for now I know that thou fearest God, seeing that thou hast not withheld thy son, thine only son, from me."—Gen. xxii. 12. If there is any difficulty in the supposition that God gave a command merely to try him, and then revoked the command, that difficulty belongs to another subject, and should not be brought in here to embarrass the point now under consideration. The plain statement is—and that is all that we have now to do with—that it was never *intended* that he should be allowed to take the life of his son; but it was meant that there should be the strongest possible trial of faith, and that, when the strength of his faith was tested, showing that he was willing to sacrifice *anything* that he had to God, and to obey *any* command, however difficult and extraordinary, the command should then be revoked. Accordingly, an arrangement was made, showing conclusively that this *was* the purpose; the arrangement by which a ram, caught in the thicket, was substituted for a sacrifice in the place of that which Abraham had expected to offer.

These are the sole facts in the narrative, and the

Scripture account is to be held responsible *only* for these.

2. The second point relates to the inquiry whether there are any principles which would show that it is conceivable that God could give such a command, or whether it does not so violate our "instincts," and all our convictions of what is right, that it would be impossible for a good man to receive such a command and to purpose to obey it. In other words, can a revelation be received as from God which contains *one* such command—one direction, issued in a solitary case, to offer up a son in sacrifice? This, it must be admitted, is a grave and difficult question.

In reply to this inquiry, it may be remarked,

(*a*) That a book pretending to be a revelation from God would *not* be received as such by mankind at large, if it contained as one of the principles of religion a general rule or law that a son—the first born, for example—was always to be offered in sacrifice. Men are undoubtedly so made that they could not believe that a command which would so violate all the instinctive feelings of their nature could be from the God who is the author of that nature. It could not be supposed that the same Being had implanted these instincts, and made them so tender and universal, and then that, in a revelation to mankind, he would make it the duty of all men habitually to disregard them. Men must believe that the laws of God are in harmony; and that what he has implanted in our very nature will not be contradicted in a real revelation of his will. Of two systems so diametrically opposed, there could not be the same author; one commanding men to love and cherish their offering, and the other commanding them to imbrue their hands in their blood. It must be admitted, therefore, that if such a command had been found in a book purporting to be a revelation from God, making it a *general* rule or requirement that the first born was to be offered in sacrifice by the hands of a father, it would not have been possible to receive it as a revelation from God, any more than it would be possible to receive a book as a revelation which should command men to commit murder or adultery, or which should require children not to honor their father or mother, or which should make falsehood and theft a duty. If, for example, the doctrine of Mr. Hume, that adultery should be practised if men would obtain all the good that can be secured in this life, or that it is no more evil to turn a few ounces of blood from its accustomed channel than any other liquid, and that therefore suicide is innocent, were found in such a book, it would be impossible for the race to receive it as a revelation from God.*

---

* Thus Mr. Hume says, in an essay which he said was, "of all his writings, historical, philosophical, or literary, incomparably the best:" "The long and helpless infancy of man requires the combination of parents for the salvation of their young; and that combination requires the virtue of CHASTITY or fidelity to the marriage bed. *Without such a utility, it will readily be owned that such a virtue would never have been thought of.*" (*Philosophical Essays,* vol. ii. p. 233. Ed. 1817.) Chastity, therefore, according to Mr. Hume, is a matter of convenience, not a matter of moral obligation.

In another place he says: "It is needless to dissemble. The consequence of a very free commerce between the sexes, and their living much together, will often terminate in intrigue and gallantry. *We must sacrifice somewhat of the useful, if we be very anxious to obtain all the agreeable qualities; and cannot pretend to reap alike every advantage.* Instances of license daily multiplying will weaken the scandal with the one sex, and teach the other by degrees to

In reference to the matter now under consideration, it may be remarked that the principle is undoubtedly laid down in the Bible that all things belong to God, and that the most choice and valuable of a man's pos-

adopt the famous maxim of La Fontaine, with regard to female infidelity, *that if one knows it, it is but a small matter; if one knows it not, it is nothing.*" (Quoted by Dr. Magee, in the work on *Atonement and Sacrifice*, p. 427. Ed. 1813.)

Thus, also, he teaches, in his Essay on Suicide, that "the life of a man is of no greater importance than that of an oyster; and, as it is admitted that there is no crime in diverting the Nile or the Danube from their courses, so he contends that there can be none in turning a few ounces of blood from their natural channel." (*Magee on Atonement and Sacrifice*, p. 429.)

Mr. Hume's doctrines on the subject of morals are thus summed up by Dr. Beattie: "That justice is not a natural, but an artificial virtue, dependent wholly on the arbitrary institutions of men, and previous to the establishment of civil society not at all incumbent; that moral, intellectual, and corporeal virtues are all of the same kind; in other words, that to want honesty, to want understanding, and to want a leg, are equally the objects of moral disapprobation, and that it is no more a man's duty to be grateful or pious than to have the genius of Homer, and the strength and beauty of Achilles; that every human action is necessary, and could not have been different from what it is; that when we speak of power as an attribute of any being, God himself not excepted, we use words without meaning; that we can form no idea of power, nor of any being endowed with power, *much less* of one endowed with infinite power; and that we can never have any reason to believe that any object or quality of an object exists of which we cannot form an idea; that it is unreasonable to believe God to be infinitely wise and good, while there is any evil or disorder in the universe, and that we have no good reason to think that the universe proceeds from a cause; that the external material world does not exist, and that if the external world be once called in doubt as to its existence, we shall be at a loss to find arguments by which to prove the being of a God, or any of his attributes; that those who believe anything certainly are fools; that adultery must be practised, if men would obtain all sessions should be devoted to God either as a thank-offering or as a burnt-offering. Under this principle, the first-born of animals, if without blemish, was to be offered in sacrifice. Ex. xiii. 2, 12; xxii. 29; xxxiv. 19; Num. iii. 13; Deut. xv. 19. This principle, if literally carried out, and if there had been no express exception, *might* have led to the inference that the first-born of children, if males, should be offered in sacrifice as well as the first-born of animals, for the *principle* that the first-born *as such* belonged to God, and should be devoted to him, was a principle that lay at the foundation of the Hebrew economy. In order, therefore, to avoid this conclusion, and to prevent the possibility of a construction which would be so much at war with every instinct of our nature, it was expressly required that the first-born *son* should be 'redeemed' by a substitute offered in his place. "And the first-born of thy sons shalt thou redeem."—Ex. xxxiv. 20. "Every firstling of an ass thou shalt redeem with a lamb; and if thou wilt not redeem it, then thou shalt break his neck:

---

the advantages of life; that if generally practised, it would soon cease to be scandalous, and that if practised secretly and frequently, it would by degrees come to be thought no crime at all; that the question concerning the substance of the soul is unintelligible; that matter and motion may often be regarded as the cause of thought; that the soul of man becomes every moment a different being, so that the actions I performed last year, or yesterday, or this morning, whether virtuous or vicious, are no more imputable to me than the virtues of Aristides are imputable to Nero, or the crimes of Nero to the man of Ross." (*Essay on the Nature and Immutability of Truth*, by Dr. Beattie, pp. 111–113.) COULD a book containing such doctrines be received as a divine revelation? Is there nothing in man which would be competent to judge on the question whether such a book could be from a pure and holy God?

and all the first-born of man among thy children shalt thou redeem."—Ex. xiii. 13. This principle was ultimately incorporated into the general arrangement that the entire tribe of Levi should be substituted in the place of the first-born of the whole people, as a tribe peculiarly set apart to the service of God. Num. iii. 13. Every precaution was, therefore, taken to *avoid* the possible conclusion in the application of a general principle, that the first-born son should be offered in sacrifice.

But does the fact that *one* such command is found in a book professing to be a revelation from God—found in the circumstances in which it is found in the Bible; so guarded that it is impossible to regard it as a general rule for mankind; so defined that it never *has* been pleaded as an argument for human sacrifice, justify the conclusion that the book cannot be from God, or that Abraham could not have received them as a command of God?

Let the following facts, then, be borne in mind: (1) God is the author of life. (2) He has a right to take it away. (3) He actually takes life away; often, too, under forms far more fearful than would have been the manner in which Isaac would have died. (4) He issues his commands to his agents to take life away: to the pestilence; to earthquakes; to storms; to diseases, most painful, loathsome, and protracted. He actually asserts the right to do this in any way that seems good to Him, *and in forms which we should have said would never have occurred under the government of a holy God.* (5) If these agents were conscious and intelligent, instead of being blind and senseless; if storms and diseases were *men*, instead of being storms and diseases, the command to close life in the manner in which they are required to do it, would be infinitely more shocking to all the sensibilities of our nature than was the command to Abraham. *Suppose* that God should issue a command to men to inflict on parts of the race all the sufferings actually brought upon mankind by the cholera, the plague, or the smallpox; suppose that this command should appear to come forth in a manner that could not be doubted, men might well stand aghast, and ask whether it was *possible* that such a command could be issued by a benevolent God, and whether anything could be sufficient to convince them that such a command came from Him, and would justify them in going forth to do this "strange work." And, if we should conceive that the diseases thus commanded to perform this work, and the elements of our nature employed in carrying the command into execution, were made conscious, might we not suppose that they would stand appalled, and ask whether it was possible that they should be commanded to execute a work that seemed so much to violate all the principles on which we naturally judge of the Maker of the worlds? The command to Abraham, in what *seems* to be severe, harsh, unnatural, bears no comparison with the command which actually goes forth from the Throne of God each day to cut down the aged and the young—the beautiful and the hopeful—the most tender and beloved of all the forms of earth—infants, daughters, wives—in the most varied and horrid forms of suffering. (6) Another remark may be made here. It will not, of course, commend itself to one class of men, and it is not of such a nature that it could be used in an argument with a sceptic—for it would be impossible to *demonstrate* that it is true, and yet it *may* be true, and in the apprehension of one who could look at things as they actually are, and who could take in the whole case, it might remove the entire difficulty. The remark is, that the whole transaction *may* have been connected with the work of redemption; that it *may* have been, in the estimation of Abraham, and in fact, a designed emblematic representation of the great sacrifice afterwards to be made for the sins of the world. The most solemn, mysterious, and momentous truth connected with the history of our world is embodied in the fact—a fact here referred to as assumed—that God gave his only Son to be a real sacrifice for the sins of the world; that he himself selected him as the victim to make expiation for human guilt; that he surrendered him to death; that he laid on him the iniquities of mankind; and that, under the appointment, and in part by the infliction of the hand of God his Father, the Redeemer bore such an amount of suffering as would be properly expressive of the value of law, and the evil of violating law. This great fact was symbolized by all the bloody sacrifices of the Hebrews, and it may have been—at least the contrary cannot be demonstrated—that it was designed, in the case of the Father of the Hebrew people, that that fact should be symbolized to his own mind in a more impressive manner than it could be by the offering of bullocks or of lambs; that an event should occur in his own history best fitted to impress his mind, and the minds of all the Hebrew people for ages, with the great truth that God, in the work of redemption, *would* give his own only-begotten Son as a sacrifice for the sins of the world; that that would, in fact, occur in the work of redemption which Abraham was commanded to represent by a symbol. A sceptic cannot *assume*, much less *demonstrate*, that the whole explanation of the transaction may not be found in this fact—and until this *is* demonstrated, it may be assumed that there *may* be an explanation, corresponding entirely with the fact, which would remove the whole difficulty. If it was a truth—a truth so exalted and mysterious as to tax the faith of the world to the utmost—that God would give his Son to be a sacrifice for sin—to suffer, to bleed, to die on a cross—it may surely be admitted as a *possible* thing, that such an amazing transaction, and one of so much interest to mankind, might be symbolized ages before it occurred by *one* event that would stand as much apart from the ordinary occurrences of life, as the atonement would in fact from the ordinary events of Providence in administering the affairs of the world. As the atonement made by the death of the Son of God stands alone in the history of the universe, it is not incredible that there should have been one event in the history of mankind so wonderful, so strange, so inexplicable, that it should be the fit representative of that which was forever thus to stand alone.

One other remark should be made in reference to the question whether the Bible commends itself to the conscience or moral sense of mankind. It is, that society, in its progress, never gets *beyond* the injunctions of the Bible in regard to morals. In fact, it never *comes up* to it. It never reaches a point where the injunctions of the Bible on the subject of honesty, liberty, benevolence, humanity, courtesy, become obsolete, or fall behind the demands of the age. It is still in advance of all the points which men have reached; and its injunctions are just as fresh, and as much adapted to the wants of man, as they were when the book was formed. The Bible was composed in a comparatively rude age of the world, and among a people comparatively unlearned. A part of it was penned not far from the age of Confucius; all of it before the time of Seneca. No small part of it was contemporary with the writings of Grecian sages and philosophers. Yet none of those writings, not those of Confucius, Plato, Seneca, *come up* to the present condition of the world. They could not be made the basis of the moral system now demanded in the position which society has assumed. To adopt them, to place society so as to be in harmony with them, would be to cause the world at once to retrograde some thousands of years, and to lose at once no small part of what it has gained in that long lapse of time. There is no plan of benevolence, however exalted in its nature, or wide in its aim, in reference to which counsel may not be found in the Bible; there is no scheme projected for the promotion of human happiness, for the extension of liberty, for meliorating the condition of the down-trodden and oppressed, to which the principles of the Bible are not applicable; and there are no laws framed for the protection of human rights, for avenging wrong, for advancing the welfare of society, the germs or principles of which may not be found in the Bible, or which, in reference to purity, benevolence, or justice, are in advance of the principles laid down in the Word of God. Books of science, like almanacs, become obsolete and useless; those which are adapted to one age are not fitted to the progress made in subsequent times. In medicine, of what use, except as historical records, and as marking the progress of the human mind, are the works of Galen and Hippocrates; in geography, of what use, except for the same purpose, are the works of Strabo, and Mela; in astronomy, the works of Ptolemy; in chemistry, the works of Roger Bacon, or of the alchemists of the middle ages? Who consults the Timæus of Plato for an account of the true origin of the universe? Who refers to Aristotle or Pliny for a just and full account of Natural History? As records of truth; as statements of science; as treatises explaining nature, these have long since ceased to be referred to, and they can never, in these respects, have the value once affixed to them. Society has gone beyond them, and will never return to the state in which they did really mark progress in the race, and contribute to the welfare of mankind. So in all the departments of morals, of law, and of learning. Our large libraries are filled with books which, like the extinct animals of the geological periods of the world, have accomplished their purpose, and are now become the 'fossils' of literature and science, rarely referred to except by some one curious in the history of man, and desirous of knowing what the world once was; as the races of the Ichthyosaurians and Megastheriums are of value only to those who would mark the progressive history of the globe. But society has not as yet gone beyond the teachings of the Bible. It has never reached a point where the Bible has not suggestions to make for the good of man in advance of all that has been done or devised. In the highest stages of human development thus far reached, it is as fresh in its counsels, as original in its instructions, as suggestive of what will be for the good of mankind, as it ever was; and in all human discoveries, in all that marks the progress of mankind, it goes before the race as the Shekinah did before the Hebrew people—a pillar of cloud by day, and of fire by night.

§ 3. *The Bible in relation to the discoveries of science.*

The subject which is here referred to is too extended to admit of being considered in the limits proposed in this Essay, even if there were no other considerations that would suggest prudence in attempting to discuss it.

A few remarks, of a general character, as illustrating the present aspect of science in its relation to revealed religion, are all which it is proper for me to attempt to make, and all which my design really demands. The question, on this point, now before the world, is, whether the statements of the Bible are contradictory to the disclosures of science?

(1) Not a few, if not all the sciences, have been arrayed against the Bible, and it has been maintained, by those who have rejected the Bible, that its statements are not reconcilable with the disclosures made by those sciences. Yet most of the objections from that source have been abandoned by infidels themselves.

Of the objections drawn from the modern astronomy, it is enough to say that they were demolished by Chalmers. Since the delivery of his celebrated "Astronomical Discourses" we have heard no more of the objection, and it will not probably be referred to by an intelligent infidel again. At one time, indeed, infidelity claimed that such stupendous plans as the Bible refers to, would not have been formed for a world so insignificant as is this. Now, it is admitted that no argument can be derived from that against revelation, but that the simple and sole inquiry is, *what in fact God has done.*

At another time it was held that the account of the origin of languages in the Bible was improbable and absurd; that the hundreds of languages and dialects on the earth could never have had a common origin, and that men could have never used the same forms of speech. There were some hundreds of languages, having, as it appeared, no affinity, no resemblance, no appearance of a common source. The account of the dispersion on the plains of Shinar was held to be ridiculous and improbable: and the book which contained such an account was held to be incredible. Without any reference to the divine origin of Christianity, this vast field of research was entered. Soon it was found, to the surprise of those who had entered on the investigation, that languages grouped themselves into families, and that the number became insensibly smaller. New affinities were discovered, and new classifications formed. The probability became stronger and stronger that there *might* have been a common origin. Sir William Jones supposed that he could trace all the languages of the world back to *three,* and subsequently it was found that science furnished strong presumption that originally there was but one. I can only refer, in a word, to the testimony of two distinguished scholars, neither of whom entered on the investigation with any intention to confirm the authority of the Bible. The first is that of Klaproth. He makes no secret of his disbelief of the Mosaic history of the dispersion, and tells us that, like many other writings of Western Asia, he regards it as a mere fable. Yet he says that, in his view, "the universal affinity of languages is placed in so strong a light, that it must be considered by all as completely demonstrated. This," says he, "does not appear explicable on any other hypothesis than that of admitting *fragments of a primary language yet to exist* through all the languages of the old and new worlds." The other witness is Herder, who also says that he regards the history of Babel as a "poetical fragment in the Oriental style." Yet he says, as the result of his investigations, that "there is great probability that the human race, and language therewith, go back to one common stock, to a first man, and not to several dispersed in different parts of the world." His conclusions do not stop here. He confidently asserts that, from the examination of languages, the separation among mankind is shown to have been violent; not, indeed, that they voluntarily changed their language, but that they were rudely and suddenly divided from one another.*

At another time, the Christian world was alarmed at the boasted antiquity of the Indies. Astronomical tables were discovered that were believed to have been formed at least 3500 years before Christ, and it was claimed by Bailly that these must be fragments of an earlier and far more perfect science. The Christian world was alarmed, and infidelity began to sound a note of triumph. The result of this may be stated in the language of Laplace—himself supposed to have no special respect for Christianity—but whose name is sufficient to settle a question of this kind. "The origin of astronomy," says he, "in Persia and India, is lost,

* Wiseman's Lectures, pp. 69, 73.

as among all other nations, in the darkness of their ancient history. The Indian tables suppose a very advanced state of astronomy; *but there is every reason to believe that they can claim no very high antiquity.*" He then proceeds to a detailed examination of the point whether the observations supposed by the Indian tables were ever actually made, and concludes that those tables were not grounded on any true observation, *because the conjunction which they suppose could not have taken place.** The objection of infidelity from those astronomical tables has been silenced, and will not be heard again.

Simultaneously with this supposed difficulty, arose one from the historical records of China and of India. The names of long lines of kings were displayed; accounts of dynasties were furnished extending back millions of ages; and it was supposed here that an objection was started to the Mosaic narrative which would be fatal. Again infidelity triumphed, and the friends of Christianity became alarmed. Yet the result here has been the same. That result is before the world; and the world—infidel and Christian—now acquiesces in the conclusion drawn by the laborious investigations of Sir William Jones, that on the most liberal construction, the existence of an established government in the East can be traced back no further than 2000 years before the Christian era, the age of Abraham, when there was already an established dynasty in Egypt, and commerce and literature were flourishing in Phœnicia. The Oriental nations have, therefore, taken their appropriate place in the history

---

* Wiseman's Lectures, p. 237.

of the world; and the objection has died away, to be heard no more.

Once more the Christian world was to be alarmed, and once more the note of triumph was to be heard for a while from infidelity. The materials for the new argument which infidelity constructed were found in Egypt. "Volney had no hesitation in placing the formation of the sacerdotal colleges in Egypt, 13,300 years before Christ, and calling that the second period of their history."* For the antiquity of Egypt, infidelity appealed to the huge and half-buried colossal images; to the subterranean temples; to the astronomical remains; and to the hieroglyphic legends of that wonderful country. In particular, an appeal was made to the zodiacs found at Dendera and Esneh, which were supposed to represent the state of the heavens at the time in which the temples where they were found were erected, and which indicated a very remote antiquity. At this period God raised up Champollion. He taught the world to read the hieroglyphics on the obelisks, the tombs, the temples of Egypt. That language, long unknown, and whose meaning it was supposed was forgotten forever, now disclosed the fact that the celebrated zodiacs extended no further back than the time of Nero or Tiberius. On one of the zodiacs he read the name of Tiberius, and on the other the name which Nero takes on his Egyptian medals. The objections from the zodiacs, the pyramids, the tombs, and the inscriptions of Egypt, lost their power forever when Champollion told the world how to read the inscription on the Rosetta stone. The objections from the

* Recherches, vol. ii. p. 440.

antiquity of India and China, and from the diversity of languages, have thus died away. Science started these objections; science solved them. The scientific world pursued these inquiries as mere matters of investigation; infidelity seized upon the results to give alarm; and again science, of its own accord, removed the difficulty.

(2) The fact that the disclosures of science on any subject cannot be reconciled with the common *interpretation* of the Bible should not be regarded as proof that they are inconsistent with the *true doctrine* of the Bible on the subject. The Bible is not responsible for the interpretations that have been affixed to it, though they may have *seemed* to be a fair interpretation, and though they may have been regarded as a part of the true faith, and as such have received the sanction of synods and councils, and have been incorporated with the creeds of the Church. It is still, and it always will be, a fair and open question whether the Bible has been fairly interpreted, and whether a more accurate knowledge of language and customs, and a more correct view of the real *design* of revelation, would not show that the statements of the Bible are wholly consistent with all the disclosures made by the telescope and by the microscope; by all the researches of the geologist, and by all the revelations of the laboratory. It can never be *assumed*, on the discovery of a new truth in science, that it is against the fair interpretation of the Bible, or that it is not possible, *by* a fair interpretation, to make its statements consistent with the disclosures of science. The first effect, on the discovery of a truth in science that *seems* to be in conflict with the Bible, should be to open the subject of *interpretation* afresh,

and to suggest the inquiry whether the Bible has been properly understood. This, of course, may lead to angry feeling, and to a charge of heresy, as it did to persecution in the time of Galileo. It may unavoidably give occasion for a *temporary* triumph of infidelity by its assuming that the current interpretation of the Bible is the correct one, and by showing, as it may easily be done, that the Bible, *as* thus currently interpreted, is contradictory to the facts made known by science. It may require time to adjust the statements of the two so that they shall harmonize; and in the mean time it may give occasion for *another* charge against the Bible that it is "a nose of wax," or "a fiddle on which any tune can be played," or that it *has* no doctrines of its own. But this is an effect which is inevitable. In due time the Bible and the facts will adjust themselves, as has been the case on the subject of astronomy. This is what must be expected to occur in a book written in a distant age; a book not designed primarily to make disclosures on this subject; a book in which the statements on this subject are incidental, and are necessarily made in the common language of men, and not in the strict technical language of science. To suppose that this could be otherwise, or to demand that it should be otherwise, would be to require that a book of revelation should, contrary to its main design, adjust all its statements on subjects in any way connected with science not to the language used in the age in which it is given, but to the technical accuracy which will be reached in the highest disclosures of science yet to be made to the world; and this would be to demand that it should *anticipate* in science all the discoveries which man could be ever expected to make, and this would be, in fact, to make the book as unmeaning as the language of the 'schoolmen' of the middle ages is now to the mass of mankind. It would be also perhaps to make it unintelligible to the present objectors to revelation, for it is conceivable that the language of science may yet, by a fuller and more accurate nomenclature, be so modified as effectually to abolish that which is now used even by the scientific world. All this would be just as reasonable as it would be to require philosophers to use the language of science in their common modes of discourse, and never again to speak of the rising or the setting of the sun, the moon, or the stars.

(3) It is clear that *if* the Bible is a revelation from God, the deductions of science and the statements of the Bible cannot be contradictory. They must ultimately harmonize. God would not make a statement in his word which would be contradicted by his works, nor cause a fact to occur in his works, the fair interpretation of which would be contrary to the statements of his word. The unbeliever undoubtedly has a right to *demand* that the statements in the Bible should be shown, by fair interpretation, to be in accordance with all the disclosures of science; and if that cannot be done, that the claims of the Bible should be abandoned. But, on the other hand, the believer has a right to *demand* that what is alleged as science shall *be* true science; that the exact facts shall be ascertained; and that it shall be understood that there is no *antecedent* presumption that the two are contradictory. He has a right to demand also that the unbeliever shall not assume that the interpretations affixed to the Bible, though they may have been the current and prevailing

interpretation for ages; though they may have received the sanction of the 'Fathers,' of synods, and of councils; though they may have been incorporated into the creeds of the Church, are the correct interpretation. It is still an open question which no one has a right to assume to be settled, what *is* the teaching of the Bible on points that are supposed to come in collision with the revelations of science. As there is no tribunal to ascertain what are the teachings of science, but as it is an open question for every man to settle for himself if he chooses, so there is no authoritative tribunal in the Church to determine what is the meaning of the Bible, but it is an open question for every man to determine as he does in regard to the meaning of any other book.

(4) In reference to by far the largest part of the sciences, it is not, and cannot be pretended that there is any contradiction between them and the Bible; in reference to most of those in which it was supposed or alleged that there was a contradiction, the point has been yielded by even the rejectors of the Bible that there is no such conflict. We have seen, in the remarks made above, that the objections drawn from astronomy, from the origin of languages, from the astronomical tables of the Hindoos, from the alleged historical records of India and China, and from the zodiacs of Egypt, have been abandoned. It is also true that in reference to the larger portion of the sciences, properly so called, it cannot be, and has never been alleged that they are contradictory to the Bible, for the Bible makes no statements in regard to them which can be supposed to come in conflict with them. This is true of the sciences

of anatomy, physiology, botany, natural history, chemistry, mental philosophy, magnetism, electricity, geometry, algebra, fluxions, metallurgy, and kindred subjects. It is also certain that in the schools and colleges of Christian countries it is rare, in the regular course of studies, that there occurs a point on which there seems to be a collision between the statements involved in the regular instruction, and the statements in the Bible, or in which it becomes necessary for a teacher who is a friend of revelation, to interpose even a single remark to guard against a perceived tendency in the science to scepticism. While this is true, it is also true that no ancient book of science on any one of these subjects, except geometry, could be used without coming into direct conflict with the statements of modern science. What would be said of the Timæus of Plato, in our colleges, in this respect? It is also true that, while no other books received by any portion of the world as a divine revelation, unless it be the Koran, could be so used without coming in direct conflict with the disclosures of science, the Bible can be used, and is used, in those schools of learning; its statements are familiarly referred to; its study is enjoined or made a matter of earnest exhortation, and with no apprehension that its statements will be found to come in collision with the regular course of instruction on these subjects, and with a conviction on the part of the friends of the Bible that the profoundest investigation of those sciences has no tendency whatever to send out into the world a generation of educated sceptics. Indeed, it is one of the sternest principles of Protestantism that the Bible *should be* in the schools of learning; it is a point on which the friends of the Bible are most readily aroused when an attempt is made to exclude it from schools and colleges; it is a point in which they feel entire confidence that the more directly and constantly they can keep that book in contact with the minds of educated and scientific men, the more certain will be its reception as a revelation from God.

(5) In respect to science, there remain some points which, it must be admitted, remain unsettled, and where it is a fair and open question still, whether the future disclosures in these sciences will accord with the revelations of the Bible. While it must be conceded by all, from the history of the past, that there is no presumption that these will not be found to accord with the statements in the Bible, it must also be conceded by the friends of revelation that it is perfectly fair for the friend of science to push his inquiries as far as he can, and with no desire to shape his facts with reference to any desired or any desirable result in their bearing on revelation. The friend of the Bible should not fear the result; the friend of science should pursue his researches as if there were no such book, and with no desire either to find it true or false. The hammer of the geologist, the blowpipe of the chemist, the glass of the astronomer, are not to be controlled or modified by any *moral* considerations.

The main points referred to here as being as yet unsettled, relate to GEOLOGY, and to THE UNITY OF THE RACE.

A. GEOLOGY.—This is a recent science. It is but a brief period since even *science* started the idea that the world is more than about six thousand years old; or, if that idea had occurred, that it has been attempted to determine it by any known facts. Fable, fancy, pretended records, had indeed referred to a long existence of nations on the earth prior to the Mosaic account of the creation of man, but no facts of science had been discovered to confirm those records, or to impart truth to those fables.

It is not proposed to enter here into any protracted inquiry on this subject. The only point *necessary* to be noticed is, that *up to this time no contradiction between the disclosures of geology and the statements of the Bible has been* DEMONSTRATED, *and that there is nothing as yet in the science which makes it certain that there will be found to be such a contradiction.*

In illustration of this, the following remarks may be made:—

(1) The science of geology must be admitted to be as yet so incomplete that it cannot be assumed to be certain in respect to those points which *seem* to be in collision with the Bible that future disclosures may not materially modify the conclusions which are to be drawn from the science. There *are*, indeed, facts in regard to the science as clearly determined as any facts in any of the other established sciences. There are facts entirely at variance with the views held formerly in regard to the past duration of the world, and with the notions heretofore entertained by the Christian world in regard to the statements of the Bible on that subject. It has been demonstrated that the world has stood many thousands, perhaps many millions of years, and the friend of revelation cannot deny this. It has been demonstrated that there were numerous orders of now extinct animals upon the earth long before the Scripture account of the creation of man—animals that have, for the most part,

long since passed away; animals adapted to a different state of things from that which now exists on the earth; animals which could not exist now. It has been demonstrated that death reigned among those animals long before man was created, and consequently that the views which have been entertained by theologians about the death of animals as connected with the transgression of man, and as the fruit of that transgression, must be abandoned. But it is yet to be proved that these points come into collision with any explicit statements of the Bible. And in reference to any supposed collision of the facts of geology with the actual statements of the Bible, it is further to be observed that the science of geology is as yet so incomplete that it is not time *yet* to affirm or to presume that the conclusions from that science, when fully settled, will be in conflict with the Bible. In a science so recent, and where the principles are as yet so imperfectly determined, and the facts so imperfectly ascertained, it does not seem too much for the friend of revelation, in cases where there may *seem* to be a conflict between the statements of the science and the statements of the Bible, to ask that the judgment should be suspended until two points are clearly settled: (*a*), until the facts in geology shall be *certainly* ascertained; and (*b*), until it shall be determined whether the fair interpretation of the Bible, not the current traditions of theology, may not be in harmony with the disclosures of the science.

(2) It is a very material fact as bearing on this subject, that, amidst all the fossil remains of the geologist, and all the records of past times, there is no proof that *man* has lived longer than the period assigned to him in

the Mosaic history. In all that the geologist relies on to demonstrate the existence of the inferior orders of animals on the earth prior to the Mosaic account of the creation of man, he has not presented us with one *human bone*, or with one indication of the existence of man. Other fossil remains, other bones, he has disinterred in abundance; but not one that has yet been proved to have belonged to the human species. So in respect to all coins, medals, historical records, monuments. There are no historical records of the existence of man on the earth that go back to such ancient times. There are no remains of unknown cities, no tombs, no mausoleums, that would prove that man then existed, now found amidst the fossil remains of extinct orders of animals. We wander among decaying ruins; we are among broken arches, pillars, tombs; we look upon the magnificent Coliseum, the mighty pyramid, the falling tower, the ivy-bound column, the ruined temple, the ancient castle; we brush the dust from ancient inscriptions, and decipher their solemn records, and make the past generations speak out amidst these monuments; but there is not a solitary voice that disputes the record of the Jewish historian about the recent origin of man, or that points to a time when he lived anterior to the bliss of Eden.

In this connection it may be proper to quote a memorable passage written by Bishop Berkley a century ago, and quoted with approbation by Sir Charles Lyell, in which he inferred, on grounds which may be termed strictly geological, the recent date of the creation of man. "To any one," says he, "who considers that, on digging into the earth, such quantities of shells, and, in some places, bones and horns of animals, are found sound and entire, after having laid there, in all probability, some thousands of years; it should seem probable that guns, medals, and implements in metal or stone, might have lasted entire, buried under ground forty or fifty thousand years, if the world had been so old. How comes it then to pass that no remains are found, no antiquities of these numerous ages preceding the Scripture accounts of time; that no fragments of buildings, no public monuments, no intaglios, cameos, statues, basso-relievos, medals, inscriptions, utensils, or artificial work of any kind, are ever discovered which may bear testimony to the existence of those mighty empires, those successions of monarchs, heroes, and demi-gods, for so many thousand years? Let us look forward and suppose ten or twenty thousand years to come, during which time we will suppose that plagues, famines, wars, and *earthquakes* shall have made great havoc in the world, is it not highly probable that, at the end of such a period, pillars, walls, and statues now in being, of granite, or porphyry, or jasper (stones of such hardness as we know them to have lasted two thousand years above ground without any considerable alteration), would bear record of these and past ages? Or that some of our current coins might then be dug up, or old walls and the foundations of buildings show themselves, as well as the shells and stones of the *primæval world*, which are preserved down to our time?"*

On this passage, Sir Charles Lyell remarks, "that many signs of the agency of man would have lasted at least as long as the 'shells of the primæval world,' had

* Alciphron, or the Minute Philosopher, vol. ii. pp. 84, 85, ed. 1732.

our race been so ancient, we may feel as fully persuaded as Berkley; and we may anticipate with confidence that many edifices and implements of human workmanship, and the skeletons of men and casts of the human form, will continue to exist when a great part of the present mountains, continents, and seas, have disappeared. Assuming the future duration of the planet to be indefinitely protracted, we can foresee no limit to the perpetuation of some of the memorials of man, which are continually imbedded in the bowels of the earth, or in the bed of the ocean, unless we carry forward our views to a period sufficient to allow the various causes of change, both igneous and aqueous, to remodel more than once the outer crust of the earth. *One* complete revolution will be inadequate to efface every monument of our existence; for many works of art might enter again and again into the formation of successive eras and escape obliteration, even though the very rocks in which they had been for ages imbedded were destroyed; just as pebbles included in the conglomerates of our epoch often contain the organized remains of beings which flourished during a prior era."*

If these things are so, how can it be believed that *man* has lived upon the earth during the ancient geologic periods of the world? What evidence is there that he existed prior to the Mosaic period of the creation? If he did exist then, how is it to be accounted for that all the monuments of his being have perished, while the memorials of other, and inferior races, remain?

---

* Principles of Geology, vol. ii. p. 157, ed. 1837.

(3) It is capable of clear demonstration that man could not have lived in the vast geologic periods of the early history of the earth; and could not, therefore, have been created but in the order of events which are described in the Mosaic narrative. The disclosures of geology all go to show that *man* was the ultimate object contemplated in creation; that all the 'types' of being previous to his appearance in the world had reference to him; that the condition of the world in those long geologic periods was such that he could not have lived then; and that when, by this long previous process, the earth was *prepared* for his residence, he then appeared, not as a development, but as a new creature. The process of this is so clear that it cannot now be doubted. Man did not appear in the early geological periods. He could not have found sustenance adapted to his nature. If he had been created then, he would have soon died. It is only at the latest stage of the development of the earth's history, as made known by geology, that the earth was fitted for the residence of man, or that he could have lived upon it. In the British Museum, almost as if by accident, and yet as the result of the researches of geological science, among the records of other ages in fossil remains, MAN is assigned exactly the place—the last in the series of creations—to which he is arranged in the Mosaic record of creation.*

All the researches of geologists have gone to confirm this fact, and to place man in the order of created things, in the exact place where Moses placed him, as the last in the series. They have gone also to show

* See the Testimony of the Rocks, by Hugh Miller, pp. 163-171.

that all the previous creations had *reference* to such a being as man, and that the progressive development in the series of created things contemplated some such being as man as the ultimate point to be reached, or had their proper termination in him. Of that fact the testimony of men whose opinions will not be called in question furnishes the fullest proof. Two such authorities, sufficient in the case, may be referred to. The one is that of Professor Owen, "supreme in his own special walk as a comparative anatomist." "The recognition of an ideal exemplar for the vertebrated animals proves," he says, "that the knowledge of such a being as man must have existed before man appeared. For the Divine Mind that planned the archetype also foreknew all its modifications. The archetypal idea was manifested in the flesh under divers modifications upon this planet, long prior to the existences of those animal species that actually exemplify it."* Not less remarkable is the testimony of Agassiz, as the result of an examination of the geologic existences, more extended and minute, in at least the department pertaining to fishes, than that of any other man. "It is evident," he says, in the conclusion of his recent work on the *Principles of Zoology*,† "that there is a manifest progress in the succession of beings on the surface of the earth. This progress consists in an increasing similarity to the living fauna, and among the verte-

---

* Quoted by Hugh Miller, "Testimony of the Rocks," p. 228.

† *Principles of Zoology*, touching the Structure, Development, Distribution, and Natural Arrangement of the Races of Animals, Living and Extinct. For the use of Schools and Colleges. Part I. Comparative Physiology. By Louis Agassiz, and Augustus A. Gould. Boston, Gould and Lincoln.

brates, especially in their increasing resemblance to man. But this connection is not the consequence of a direct lineage between the faunas of different ages. There is nothing like parental descent connecting them. The fishes of the Palæozoic age are in no respect the ancestors of the reptiles of the Secondary age, nor does man descend from the mammals which preceded him in the Tertiary age. The link by which they are connected is of a higher and immaterial nature, and this connection is to be sought in the view of the Creator himself, whose aim in forming the earth, in allowing it to undergo the successive changes which geology has pointed out, and in creating successively all the different types of animals which have passed away, *was to introduce man upon the globe.* MAN IS THE END TOWARDS WHICH ALL THE ANIMAL CREATION HAS TENDED FROM THE FIRST APPEARANCE OF THE FIRST PALÆOZOIC FISHES." No one can fail to remark how entirely this accords with the account of the creation of man in the first chapter of the book of Genesis, and with the statement of the place and importance of man everywhere found in the Bible.

(4) It is certain that this fact, thus stated as the result of the investigations of geology—the fact that man is the *last* in the series of created beings; that he had no place upon the earth in the earlier periods of its history; that he was not found among the animals first made; that he could not have existed in those periods; and that all the previous creations had a reference to him, and terminated on him as the highest type of being on earth, could have been known to Moses, if they are fairly implied in his statement, only as the result of revelation. It cannot be pretended that he was acquainted

with the revelations of that science which has been, as yet, last in the order of human investigation—geology; and it cannot be believed that his statement was the result of a happy conjecture. Such a conjecture is found nowhere else in the writings of men; it is one which sceptics now are unwilling to believe to be true, and the correctness of which they are constantly endeavoring to set aside. It is a statement, therefore, which, when found in a book professing to be a revelation, could have been only the result of a knowledge superior to any that man possessed from any other source. It is, however, such a statement as, on the supposition that the Bible is of divine origin, and that God, the Author of the Book, knew, as he must certainly have known, that these discoveries in geology would be made in a far distant age of the world, might have been reasonably expected to be found there, for it must have been foreseen that a comparison would be made between the revelations of geology and the statements of the Bible in regard to the origin of man, which would have an important bearing on the question whether the Bible is from God.

(5) There is one other consideration which *should* be allowed to exert an important influence in determining the question whether the disclosures of geology are consistent with the statements of the Bible. This consideration may be thus stated and illustrated: In the courts of justice, the testimony of medical men is often called in, not to determine in regard to the question whether life has been taken where one has been accused of murder, but to determine the question whether what may have been administered to the murdered man was poison, and was sufficient in quan-

tity to take his life; or whether the blow which may have been struck, was of sufficient force, or so affected a vital part, as to destroy life. In such a case, the medical man may know nothing of the facts as to the question who administered the poison, or who inflicted the blow, and consequently may have no evidence to give as to the question whether the man accused is the one really guilty of the crime, but he gives his testimony on a point in which he *is* qualified to judge, and where the court and jury may *not* be qualified to judge. That is, the court calls in the aid of his medical knowledge and experience in a case where the witness would be impartial, and where his knowledge may be of the utmost value in forming an opinion. Those who usually occupy the position of judges would not be supposed to be qualified to determine these points for themselves; those who are commonly called to act on a jury are wholly incompetent. To this mode of appeal there can certainly be no objection; and no one supposes that injustice is likely to be done, even if the decision of the case should turn finally in fact on this testimony.

Something like this must occur in regard to the questions respecting the relation of geology to the Bible. While no man would say that the geologist, as such, is to determine the question whether the Bible is a revelation from God; while no one would maintain that it is to be received by mankind because one geologist sees no discrepancy between the two, or rejected because another geologist thinks he does; while the great principle is to be held firm that every man is to judge for himself whether *he* can receive the Bible as a revelation, it is still true that the great mass of men are wholly unable to determine the questions respecting geology, as they are those which pertain to other sciences. They are not acquainted with the facts of the science. They have not the ability or the opportunity to investigate those facts, and they never can, for themselves, institute an intelligent comparison between those doctrines and the statements of the Scriptures. They are as ignorant of those facts as they are of the higher revelations of astronomy; as ignorant as the jury in the cases supposed is on the question whether what was administered was poison of such a nature, and in such a quantity, as to take life, or whether the wound inflicted was the real cause of the man's death. In the questions suggested by geology, therefore, in regard to revelation, it does not seem improper to ask what is the impression made on the minds of geologists themselves, and whether the most profound and extended acquaintance with the science has *in fact* had a tendency to make those who are most learned in this science, and best qualified to judge, infidels. The fair question is not whether there may be found geologists who are unbelievers, for there are undoubtedly such men, as there are astronomers, anatomists and historians, who are sceptics in religion. And the question, furthermore, is not whether such geologists have been made infidels, or have been confirmed in their infidelity by the study of geology, for this *may* have been the case, as it is undoubtedly true that an infidel astronomer, anatomist, or historian might endeavor to confirm himself in scepticism by facts drawn from his favorite science, and that he may have pursued the science itself in such a manner as to have led him into scepticism. But the proper question in all such cases is, *whether the study of these sciences has in fact had a tendency to make men infidels;* whether those most eminent in these departments of knowledge have been led to reject the authority of revelation from the disclosures of their own sciences; and whether the fact that a part of their number are sceptics cannot be fairly traced to some other cause than to the *necessary* conclusions drawn from their own favorite sciences. It seems to be plain that the fact that such men as Galileo, Kepler, and Newton did not see any discrepancy between the teachings of astronomy and the Bible; that so large a portion of astronomers are believers in the Bible; and that the highest disclosures of astronomy are made a part of the regular instruction in all Christian colleges, without any apprehension of the result as bearing on revealed religion, should be regarded as furnishing some evidence on which minds not competent to make the investigation themselves might rely, that there *is* no discrepancy between the Bible and the revelations of astronomy.

Now, there are undoubtedly geologists who are infidels, as there are anatomists, astronomers, chemists, historians, who are. But while this is true, it is also true that the great body of geologists are *not* infidels; that the men whose names have been most distinguished in prosecuting that science are *not* rejecters of the Bible; and that the Christian world, by admitting the study of geology into its colleges and schools, is *not* treating the subject as if it were felt that there is anything to be dreaded from the cultivation of that science. It is sufficient here, in order to show the nature of this argument, to refer to the names John Pye Smith, Prof. Buckland, Prof. Silliman, Prof. Richard Owen, Pres.

Hitchcock, and Hugh Miller. That such men do not see any such discrepancy between the statements of the Bible and the disclosures of geology as to shake their faith in revelation, may be allowed to furnish evidence to minds not competent to make the investigation themselves, that there is little danger that any conclusions yet to be reached from the science will be likely to militate against the statements of the word of God.

It is a consideration also which should be allowed to have no little weight on a question of this nature, and in the point of view now under consideration, that without an exception at present, all the colleges, and a very large part of the academies and schools for both sexes in this land, have been either founded directly for the promotion of Christianity in connection with sound learning, or are under Christian influence; that a large portion of the presidents, professors, and teachers in those schools are ministers of the Gospel or private members of the church; and that geology is taught as a part of the system of regular instruction as freely as any other branch of learning. No apprehension is felt that the fair conclusions from that science will be found to be in conflict with the revelations of the Bible. No such contradiction has been established between the two as to excite alarm among the friends of religion. The *presumption* from such facts as these is that there *is* no such contradiction between the two.

B. The Unity of the Race.—The questions which have arisen out of this subject are, like those of geology, of recent origin. Until within quite a recent period, it has not been seriously maintained to any considerable extent that the different classes of men upon the earth have had a different origin; or that there was any discrepancy between the facts on that subject, as ascertained by science, and the teachings of the Bible. It has been supposed that all the diversities in complexion, in the hair, in the facial angle, in the anatomical structure, could be accounted for on some other theory than that the races have had each a separate ancestry, or consistently with the doctrine that all the families of men have been derived from one pair.

This point has assumed an importance in this age which it has never had before, and it cannot but have an important bearing on the question respecting the truth of the Bible, as well as on the subject of freedom and slavery—for there seem to be but two considerations which could make any class of men *desire* to find that there has been a diversity of origin in regard to the races of mankind: One, that the Bible may be found to be false in its statements; the other, that there may be some plausible pretext to justify one part of mankind in enslaving another. If, in the one case, it could be demonstrated that the races of men have had a diversity of origin, that fact would destroy the authority of the Bible, for, as we shall see, the statements in the Bible on that subject are explicit; if, in the other case, the fact of such a diversity of origin could be established, it would be one of the readiest ways of justifying the enslaving of the inferior order of human beings by the superior, or, at least, it would destroy one of the most troublesome arguments which has been urged against the system of slaveholding, that which is derived from the fact that "God has made of one blood all the nations of men," or that the slave and his master are brethren.

In reference to the question about the unity of the race, there are two things to be stated which must be admitted to be true alike by the friends and the enemies of the Bible.

One is, that the question in regard to the origin of the races, is, *as a scientific question, as yet unsettled.* It is not so determined as to command the universal, or even the general assent of scientific men, that the races of men have had a different origin, or that all the diversities of complexion and of anatomical structure cannot be accounted for on the supposition that all are descended from one pair. The great mass of scientific men are not, in fact, convinced of this, nor has the doctrine that the race has had a diversity of origin *yet* passed into the admitted facts of science. It cannot be assumed, therefore, that the facts in the case are contrary to the statements in the Bible.

The other point that must be admitted is, that it is a perfectly fair and open scientific question whether there *is* evidence that the races have had a diversity of origin, or whether all existing facts *can* be explained on the supposition that the race has descended from one pair. As in the case of geology, astronomy, anatomy, and all the other sciences, the inquiry on this subject may be pursued, and must be pursued, in a manner quite independent of the testimony of the Bible, and with no fear, on the one hand, of impinging on its doctrines, and with no desire, on the other, as a purely scientific pursuit, to find the testimony of the Bible true. The scientific man should not *desire* to reach any favorite conclusions unfavorable to a belief in the divine origin of the Bible, nor should the friend of the Bible *dread* to have the inquiry pursued on the most independent scientific principles.

With these views, it may not be improper to state exactly how the matter on this point now stands, and what is the probability thus far, that any results will be reached which will be in conflict with the statements in the Bible about the origin of man.

What seems necessary to be stated on this subject, so far as it relates to the question about the unity of the race in its bearing on the truth of the Bible, may be conveniently arranged under four heads:—

I. It is an unquestionable doctrine of the Bible that the whole race of mankind is descended from one original pair—Adam and Eve; or that there has *not* been a separate ancestry for each of the subordinate races of men—the Mongolian, the Caucasian, the Ethiopian, and the American. I believe that the Bible asserts that. I believe that he who receives the Bible is bound to hold that doctrine. I believe that the rejecter of the Bible has a right to hold him who professes to believe the Bible *to* that doctrine. I believe that the statements of the Scriptures on that point are so clear, and that the doctrine of the unity of the race as descended from one pair is so implied in all the statements of the Bible about man—so identified with all the doctrines of the Bible in regard to the Fall and the Redemption of man—that *if it could be demonstrated that the human family is* NOT *descended from one pair, and is* NOT, *in the proper sense of the term, one race, it would be impossible to receive the Bible as a revelation from God.* I can conceive of no fair method of interpretation which would make the teachings of the Bible consistent with such a fact.

In support of this opinion that the Bible teaches that the race is one, as descended from one pair, I refer to the following considerations:—

(1) The account in the Book of Genesis supposes this. In that statement (ch. i.) there is a general account of the preparation of the earth to be the abode of the different races of animated beings. There is a statement of the creation of fowls, and fishes, and mammalia, without specifying any distinct location, or any distinct specific parentage, with *general* statements only. "Let the *earth* bring forth grass." "Let *the waters* bring forth abundantly the moving creature that hath life, and the fowl that may fly above the earth." "Let *the earth* bring forth the living creature after his kind, cattle and creeping thing, and beast of the earth after his kind." In these statements ample room is left for the supposition that they may have been brought into existence in the seas, the rivers, the forests, the deserts, the air, or the waters where they may now be found. But in the account of the creation of *man*, there is a specific statement of the formation of one pair of human beings; located in a particular spot; placed under a particular form of administration; and sustaining a particular relation to the inhabitants of the newly made world. This is the whole account of the creation of *man* in the Bible. It teaches that one pair was formed by the act of the Creator, and as the *last* act of creation. The account implies that no other human beings were made; the account is inconsistent with the supposition that there were any other such creations.

(2) The Bible teaches that the flood swept off the race—*all* human beings save one family. On this point, the teaching of the Scriptures is perfectly unambiguous. Whether the flood swept over the whole *earth* or not, it swept off all the races of men. No one can doubt that Moses meant to declare that all human beings, except the one family of Noah, were cut off by the deluge. This is perfectly clear, not only from the general account in the narrative, but by the declaration that is made after that family had left the ark: "These are the three sons of Noah, and of them was *the whole earth* overspread."—Gen. ix. 19. No man can possibly receive the account in Genesis as true, and yet suppose that there were, in any part of the earth, during the flood, surviving races or families of human beings—races of another origin, that were not cut off in the deluge. If, therefore, there had been originally different founders of the races, or different races of men at the creation, they were, according to the Scripture account, swept off at the deluge; if the present inhabitants of the earth are of different races, there has been, somewhere upon the earth, a process of creation since the days of Noah, if the account of the flood be true.

(3) The account in the Bible is that the earth was peopled from the family that survived the flood. There is no record of any new creation of men; there is no room left to suppose that such an act of creation occurred. One of the most remarkable portions of history to be found anywhere, is the tenth chapter of the Book of Genesis. It seems, to a casual reader, to be among the most dry and unimportant documents that have come down to us from ancient times, being almost wholly made up of names, and apparently bar-

ren of incident and interest; and yet, barren as it is, it contains more information about the origin of nations and the peopling of the world, and does more to explain the state of affairs where history properly *begins*, than all the Chinese, the Chaldean, the Greek, and the Roman historians put together. That one chapter makes clear in history what would otherwise be unintelligible, and explains what would otherwise be involved in impenetrable mystery. That chapter supposes that the world was peopled by the descendants of one family; and it is a remarkable fact that the origin of all the nations whose source can be ascertained at all, can be traced up to some of the branches of that one family. If history has had any other records of the origin of *any* of the present dwellers upon the earth, that history is not now accessible, and it may be presumed to be irrecoverably lost. There *is* no other account of the origin of man than that which is found in Genesis; and that account supposes that there is but one race of men upon the earth.

(4) The account of the origin of sin and death in the Bible supposes the same thing. The reason why all men sin is distinctly traced to the sin of one man; and death is everywhere declared to be the effect of sin. Whatever force men may attribute to the statement, whether they are disposed to receive it as credible or not, the statement in the Bible is unambiguous, that sin and death in *man* are to be traced to the fact that Adam, as the head of the race, violated the law of God, and incurred its penalty. The Scripture doctrine is, that "in Adam all die" (1 Cor. xv. 22); that "by one man sin entered into the world, and death by sin" (Rom. v. 12); that "by one man's disobedience many were

made sinners" (Rom. v. 19); and that "by man came death" (1 Cor. xv. 21). It will be seen, at once, that though men universally sin and die, this would not be a correct or satisfactory explanation of those facts, if there are different races of men that have been created at different times. If any portion of human beings belong to another race than that of Adam, it is no explanation of the fact that *they* sin and die to say that *he* violated the law of God. Whatever force that reason may have, it bears only on those who belong properly to his own posterity. It should be added here, also, that whatever may be thought of this explanation of the fact that sin and death have come upon the race, no other explanation has been furnished.

(5) The work of redemption is founded on the supposition that there is one race. Christ assumed human nature, and died for men. He is expressly spoken of as the "second man" (1 Cor. xv. 47); "the last Adam" (1 Cor. xv. 45), in contradistinction from "the first man," and "the first Adam." He comes to repair the ruins of the fall; to meet the consequences of the sin of the parent of mankind; to lay a foundation for the offer of pardon and salvation to all who were ruined by the apostasy in Eden. Thus it is said, "As in Adam all die, even so in Christ shall all be made alive" (1 Cor. xv. 22); "by man came death, by man came also the resurrection of the dead" (1 Cor. xv. 21); "as is the earthy, such are they that are earthy, and as is the heavenly, such are they also that are heavenly" (1 Cor. xv. 48); "as we have borne the image of the earthy, we shall also bear the image of the heavenly" (1 Cor. xv. 49); "as by one man's disobedience many were made sinners, so by the obedience of one shall many be made

righteous" (Rom. v. 19), and "where sin abounded, grace did much more abound" (Rom. v. 20). Thus, also, the command is given to go and preach the gospel to every creature, *on the ground* that Christ died for all, or tasted death for every man. Nor can it be denied that all this—the creation, the fall, the atonement; sin, woe, death, redemption—proceeds on the supposition that the race is *one;* that Christ took upon him human nature as such, and died for man as such, with reference to no particular race, or family of man. The offer of the gospel to any one supposes that *he* is a descendant of the apostate Adam, and *therefore* involved in sin and misery; to no one would it be proper to offer that gospel *except* on that supposition; from no one have we a right to withhold it if that supposition is true.

(6) It is expressly affirmed in the Bible that there is one race: "And hath made of one blood all nations of men for to dwell on all the face of the earth."—Acts xvii. 26. The fair and natural meaning of this is that the nations of the earth belong to one race, or are descended from one parentage. If this is not true, Paul could not with any propriety have made the assertion as he did. His design in thus addressing the people of Athens cannot be mistaken. It was to prepare the way for what he intended to say about the gospel, that it was needed by all, and was adapted to all. If there are different races of men, Athens would have been the very place to announce that fact. It had twenty thousand freemen, and four hundred thousand slaves. It would have been an eminently popular doctrine to have announced to Stoics and Epicureans that they were of nobler blood, and had a different origin, from the slaves

beneath them. But Paul hinted at nothing of this; he evidently believed nothing of this; he taught a doctrine which cannot be reconciled with this.

The sum of what has been said in this argument is that the Bible proceeds on the supposition that there was one pair which was the head of all human beings; that there is an impassable distinction between the human race and all other dwellers upon the earth; that all human beings in all lands and ages are affected by the conduct of the first man *as if* all were descended from him; that one Saviour, descended in his human nature from him, is provided for all; that the same gospel, and on the same grounds, is offered to all; that the same "blood" flows in all human veins.

II. The same fact in regard to the unity of the race is confirmed by the testimony of history, so far as historical records bear on the subject.

The authentic records of history trace up the affairs of no one of the great divisions of the race to any other ancestors than the Adam and Eve of the Scriptures. They may not, indeed they do not, all trace up the affairs of the race *to* this ancestry; but they disclose no other. If they do *not* go up to this, they are lost in fables, myths, and shadows. This argument lies essentially in these three points:—

First, in the fact that all authentic records of the human race lie *within* the period assigned by Moses as that when man was created. Indeed, no well authenticated history goes back over three-quarters of that period, and when we have gathered all that can be gathered of history from profane records and monuments, there is a long period after the creation of man in which the Bible is the sole guide. No one can penetrate that dark region farther than the Jewish historian leads him; no one, therefore, can appeal to any *records* which will disprove the truth of that in the Bible.

Second. We have in the Bible a designed historical account of the creation of man—of man as man. This account occurs at the close of the account of the creation of other beings, the *last* work of creation on the earth. It is designed to be a record of the creation of *man* as distinct from the account of the creation of the inhabitants of the sea, the dry land, and the atmosphere. It is a remarkably clear and distinct account; and accords, in all the circumstances, so far as we can judge, with what must be true. It gives an account of the formation of the body out of what is called 'the dust of the ground,' that is, the same material, or as we should say, the same *chemical* substances of which other things are composed, in entire accordance with what we now know to be the fact; and of the imparting of the breath of life, the immortal nature, from a higher source, the divine Spirit itself, in accordance with what we find all men to be endowed with. It gives an account of the formation of a single pair, sustaining a relation to each other in their *origin* which accords with the laws of our nature respecting the marriage relation, and which gives the highest sanction and importance to that relation. In the account of the origin of this one pair, it has stated a fact which will explain the peopling of the world, for no one will doubt that the world, so far as numbers are concerned, may have been peopled as it has been from that one original pair. This history is clear, distinct, unambiguous, and it goes up to the beginning of things.

Third. This is the *only* account which we have of the creation of a human being. As already intimated, no other history *pretends* to give any account that would be satisfactory to a philosophical mind that can contravene this. In all *authentic* history—history that is in the least degree entitled to credence—as that of Egypt, Babylonia, Greece, Rome, India, and China, we find, at the earliest periods to which they go back, human beings already in existence playing their part in human affairs—building cities, cultivating fields, founding empires, waging war; we find no account of the creation of a new race there to perform an allotted work in that particular land. Travellers furnish no account of the creation of men now in any new portion of the world; and in all the records of ancient and modern times that have any claim to credibility, there *is* no account of the creation of more than one pair; there is no other head of the races of men than the Adam and Eve of Moses; there is no starting up of a new order of beings upon the earth.

III. The *moral* argument for the unity of the human race goes to confirm these views. This argument is based on what we find in man, as man, showing that there is one family, and that man is wholly distinct from all other orders and species of beings upon the earth; that is, showing that there is such a uniformity and unity as to mark a common origin. I refer here to the following points:—

First, to the fact that all men have *reason*—as all *would* have if descended from the one original pair—as no dwellers on the earth *do* have who do not belong to this family. It is true that God might create any number of rational beings quite isolated from each other and independent of each other; but the point now urged is, that the race of man has this peculiar endowment *as* if all were descended from a first pair. All men are so far alike in this that they *seem* to belong to one family; they are so unlike all other creatures on the earth in this respect, that they *seem* to have had a separate and distinct origin from them. This attribute of reason is the same in all men—the same in kind, if not in degree. It places a vast and impassable barrier between man and all other creatures. Not one of them ever approximates it as it is in man; not any class of human beings ever, in this respect, sink so low as to be incapable of distinction from the orders of the brute creation. If one in human form is born bereft of this —an idiot—we feel at once assured that he has not come up to the dignity of his race; that though he has the *form*, he has not that which most properly belongs to man: and in seeing one thus possessed of the form of man, but destitute of that which properly characterizes man, we have a deeper impression of the difference between man and all other creatures on earth than we ever do in comparing any of the brute creation with man. Humble as the lot of the idiot is, we never confound him with the ourang outang, or with any of the monkey tribe. He belongs to a race that was made to be endowed with reason, and our compassion towards him is excited not by the fact that he is destitute of reason—for so is the horse and the ox—but by the fact that, being designed for a more exalted purpose, he has, in this respect, sunk to the level of the brute. There is always a marked distinction between the feelings which we have towards him and towards any of the brute creation.

It may be that these cases of idiocy are permitted to occur partly *in order* that rational man may see how far God has elevated him in the scale of being, and what a difference there is, and must be, between his proper rank and that of all the inferior races.

Second. All human beings have *conscience*, and no others have. It is admitted here, also, that God *might* create any number of isolated and independent beings, endowed with this faculty; but the remark now made is, that where we find a certain class endowed thus, and separated from all others by an impassable chasm, it is most philosophical to refer them to a common origin, and to suppose that they belong to one race. Now no one will doubt that man, as such, is endowed with conscience, and that as such he is separated by an interval that is never crossed, from all other creatures on the earth. It is doubtful whether in any other creature on earth there is even the slightest *glimmering* of this faculty, or anything which would ever suggest it as even a possible thing. The domestic dog is the only animal that ever *seems* to make any approximation to a consciousness of having done wrong; and if in that animal it ever exists, it is in the slightest possible degree, and wholly incapable of cultivation in the species. In man, however, it is universally found in the Caucasian, the Mongolian, the Ethiopian, the American. It may be much darkened, obscured and perverted, but it is there, and it is capable, by cultivation, of becoming all that is needful to control, restrain, and govern human conduct. It lives and lingers amidst the deepest debasement, and a human being can never be so degraded that it shall be wholly expelled from the bosom. We are as certain of finding it, in some form, in the most debased savage as in him who has reached the highest type of civilization; in the most oppressed slave, as in the most exalted freeman. We are sure that it is there; we are sure that it can be aroused so as to become a most powerful agent in restraining from sin, and prompting to virtue. Now it is the most natural and philosophical interpretation of this fact, to infer that where this exists, there *is* one race. It is such a fact as would exist if the race were one; it cannot well be supposed that God would engage in separate and independent works of creation, when this is found so prominent, so powerful, and so distinctive a faculty.

Third. As connected with this, and as consequent on this, man is a being, as such, capable of being governed by moral law. Here it is to be admitted, also, that God *might* have made any number of beings isolated and independent, who would be capable of being governed by moral law; but the point now suggested is, that where this is found as constituting a distinct class of beings, it is most natural and philosophical to suppose that they had a common origin and a common ancestry. It cannot be denied that there is a class of undoubted facts on which this argument is predicated. Man is the only being on earth capable of being governed by moral law, or in relation to whose conduct this can be relied on. Man *is* so governed. The laws of God; the laws of conscience; the laws of morals; the sense of right and wrong, of justice and injustice—these and kindred things are the main grounds of reliance all over the world in the government of man. In the worst forms of despotism; under the most vigilant and rigid police; in an army—the most arbitrary and absolute of all governments; in all forms of slavery, there is a reliance for securing virtue, order, and industry, derived from the sense of moral obligation, tenfold more constant and more powerful than there is from force or fear. Under free institutions it is almost the *only* reliance, and if we take any instance that may occur under the most absolute form of despotism, we should be surprised, perhaps, to find in how many respects comparatively the conduct of the subject is secured by the operations of conscience, and by a sense of what is right; in how few, though these may be more marked and prominent, by the dread of punishment. Whatever there is of fidelity in the domestic relations; of kindness to others; of honesty and truthfulness; of temperance, chastity, and charity—nay, of obedience to laws though unjust, and of respect to the despot himself, is to be traced much more to this sense of right and wrong than to mere arbitrary power. But for this no government could be instituted over man; no subordination could be secured. And this pertains to man alone. We expect to find it everywhere; we make it an element in all our calculations about a human being. We *cannot* make it an element in our calculations about any *other* creature on earth. Now this looks *as if* the race were one; *as if* there was something that divided this one race absolutely and forever from all inferior beings. It is just such an arrangement as *would* exist on the supposition that all men are descended from one ancestry; it is a fact which cannot be easily explained on any *other* supposition.

Fourth. The endowments of man in reference to the future all show the same thing. I mean that there is a class of endowments in this respect to be found in man, and in man alone, which are what they would be on the supposition that the race is descended from a single pair, and which are such as they would *not* be on any other supposition. I refer to the fact that human beings have hopes, desires, and aspirations, which other creatures have not, and that they are of such a character as to indicate a common origin. These endowments may be, indeed, very feeble in many cases. They may be overlaid by ignorance; by corrupt passions; by brutality. They may be almost trodden out by the heel of oppression. But they exist. They can be revived. They may become powerful in any human being. We have only to *cultivate* them, to place men in such circumstances that they may be developed, to make these endowments most elevated and most transforming elements in controlling men. And these things exist in man alone. In no other creature, by any process of cultivation, or by any length of years, can the glimmerings of these feelings be excited; nor can the most elevated of the brutal creation be placed, in these respects, on a level with the very lowest of the human species. Is not the most natural explanation of this fact the supposition that all the race has descended from one pair?

Fifth. It is also an indisputable fact, indicating unity in the race, that the distinction between man and the lower animals in the points now referred to, is never confounded. The line which divides them is never crossed. The brute never becomes a man. The faculties of the brute are never so enlarged or developed that he is exalted to the condition of a human being, that he reasons, acts from conscience, cherishes hopes, builds houses, writes books, makes speeches, constructs railroads, bridges, or telegraphs. He makes no attainment which he transmits to coming ages; he does nothing which makes the instinct of the next generation of his own species different from what it was in the first one of the race. The beaver built his house with as much skill, and the honey-bee its cell with as much mathematical accuracy, in the first age of the world, as the beaver and the bee of the present generation do. The lion and the elephant of the early ages is a lion or an elephant still, and nothing has been done to change either of them into a man.

It is true that this consideration would not of itself demonstrate that all the race is descended from one pair, any more than a similar consideration would demonstrate that all the lions, or all the wolves, or all the elephants were descended respectively from one pair; but it is a consideration to show that there is *unity* in the race; that it is separated by impassable barriers from all the races of animals beneath; and that the most natural solution of the facts in the case is that they all had one origin.

Sixth. To this conclusion not a few of the most eminent men in science have come as the result of purely scientific investigation. It is not to be denied that a different opinion is embraced by other men, some of them also eminent in science; but the fact now adverted to may be regarded as a proof that the doctrine of a diversity of origin of the human race is not an *established* fact in the purely scientific world, and cannot be alleged as an argument to overthrow the authority of the Bible. He cannot be properly accused of credulity, or of disregarding the conclusions of science, who maintains with such men as

11

will now be referred to the doctrine of the unity of the human race, and the belief of the Scripture account that all the varieties of men on the earth have descended from one pair.

"The different races of mankind," says Humboldt —employing the language of the distinguished German naturalist Müller, to give expression to the view which he himself adopts—"the different races of mankind are not different species of a genus, but forms of one sole species." "The human species," says Cuvier, "appears to be single." "When we compare," says Pritchard, "all the facts and observations which have been heretofore fully established as to the specific instincts and separate physical endowments of all the distinct tribes of sentient beings in the universe, we are entitled to draw confidently the conclusion that all human races are of one species and one family."*

IV. It has not *yet* been shown that the diversities among men cannot be accounted for on the supposition that all the varieties of the human race have been derived from one pair. It is not easy, indeed, to prove a negative, and it is not ordinarily fair in logic to call on an adversary to demonstrate a negative, yet, in this case it is certainly fair to demand that he who denies that all men are descended from one pair, and that the Scripture account is the true one, should demonstrate that the varieties in the human race CANNOT be accounted for, except on the supposition of a diversity of origin. This is the essential point of his position. There is certainly no historical fact on which he can rely to demonstrate that the varieties of men on the

* Testimony of the Rocks, pp. 265, 266.

earth have had a different parentage; there are no documentary records—no monuments—no, not even any traditions—which go back to any distant parentage of the Caucasian, the Mongolian, the African, and the American races; for there *are* no records which go up to the origin of man, unless those records are found in the Bible. With all the testimony, therefore, which history actually furnishes that men are descended from one pair; with all the presumptions in favor of that fact derived from the considerations which have been suggested above; with the undoubted fact that very material changes *are* made in men, and in the habits, the form, the qualities of the lower animals, by climate, by training, by accident, it is not improper to demand of him who denies that the races of men are descended from one pair, that he should demonstrate that the diversities existing among men CANNOT have been produced by influences such as have been referred to; and particularly the three following *possible* solutions—to specify no more—must be set aside, or shown to be impossible, before it will be proper to draw the conclusion that the Scripture account is false:—

(1) It must be shown that the varieties in the human family, in complexion, stature, and anatomical structure, *cannot* have been the result of climate, or of long-continued habits and customs. Very great changes, in these respects, *are* produced by these causes; and it is necessary that it should be shown that the acknowledged differences among men lie *beyond* the range of such changes. It might be necessary, also, to show *how far* such causes may go, and where exactly is the dividing line between what may be produced, and what not, from those causes. There are great varieties among the Mon-

golian people themselves, and yet it would hardly be maintained that the Tartars, and the Hindoos, and the Chinese races have each a separate ancestry. There are great varieties in the American races of savages, and yet it would not be maintained that each of the tribes which constituted the Iroquois, the Mexicans, the Peruvians, and the Patagonians, had a separate ancestry. There are very great varieties in the African races between the inhabitants of Congo, the Bakwains, and the Caffrarians, but it has not been held to be necessary to suppose that each of these varieties had a different ancestry. Even the advocates of a diversity of origin in the human race, have supposed that all these subordinate varieties can be accounted for on a different supposition than that they each had a separate ancestry. It is not improbable that the hundred and fifty varieties of *dogs* on the earth could be traced to a single pair; and can it be shown that the varieties in the human species *could* not be accounted for on the supposition that the causes above referred to might have produced it? This MUST be demonstrated—not asserted—before it will be logical to set aside the testimony of the Bible in the case.

(2) It must be demonstrated by him who denies the doctrine that all the races of men have descended from one pair, that the varieties which exist could not have been the result of what is commonly called "accident:" that is, a variety which, so far as human knowledge can go, can be traced to no known cause—a variety producing a new type or form, which may be propagated or transmitted to future generations. There can be no doubt that there *are* laws in regard to such methods of producing variety in plants and animals;

but man, as yet, has been unable, to any extent, to arrange and classify those laws. Yet it is to this, more than to anything else, perhaps, that we owe the varieties in the vegetable and animal kingdoms, on which the happiness of man and the progress of the world so much depend. Under this law, if it is a law, and not the result of a direct divine interference, the *species* are continued intact in the vegetable and animal kingdoms; the proper lines between orders and species are never crossed; the great divisions between the different kingdoms are never confounded; but within these limits, endless *varieties* are introduced upon the earth, rendering it possible that there should be a constant *advance* in human things. What seems to be an accident in the races of horses, sheep, cattle, by which one or more of a superior order, or of a different color or form, may be produced and propagated, becomes the foundation for the different breeds of horses, sheep, and cattle; and *to* this fact, undoubtedly, is to be traced the origin of the different breeds of animals, and the fact that those of one generation may be so much more valuable than those of a former age. It is a well known fact, also, that in planting the seeds of apples, strawberries, peaches, and other fruits, there is no certainty, nor indeed the smallest probability, that any considerable number of seeds will produce the same fruit as the parent. While there will be no crossing between the species; while the apple will produce an apple, the peach a peach, and the strawberry a strawberry, and nothing else, it is still true that none of them may be like the parent, and that no two of the same kind of seeds will produce the same kind of fruit. It is to this, as is well known, that we obtain from "*seedlings*" that vast variety of fruit which we now possess; and from this fact it occurs that there is a possibility of *progress* in the cultivation of fruit and grain. A strawberry, a peach, an apple, thus produced, may be far in advance in size and flavor of the parent, and, by becoming the parent of a new variety, may lay the foundation for permanent progress in horticulture or agriculture. The products of "seedlings," also, are capable of propagation. While it is true, as a general law, that the "hybrids," the "cross-breeds," and the "half-breeds," are less susceptible of propagation, and soon "run out;" and while it is true that the offsprings of different races of animals cannot propagate their kind, this is by no means true of the *accidental varieties in the same species.* Now it cannot be *demonstrated* that all the varieties in the human race may not have been produced under some such law; or, in other words, that they may not be the result of an accidental variety, as difficult of explanation as the existence of a black sheep in a flock; or a horse of peculiar color, beauty, or size; or of a Devon, an Ayrshire, or a Durham variety among cattle; or of Hovey's Seedling, the Moyamensing Pine, the McAvoy's Superior, the British Queen, or the Early Scarlet, among strawberries; or of the Early Harvest, the Summer Pearmain, the Maiden's Blush, the Hawthornden, the Rambo, the Fall Pippin, the Bell-flower, the Greening, or the Spitzenberg, among apples; or of the Carnation, the Elton, the Kentish, the Late Duke, the May Duke, the Morello, or the White Heart, among cherries; or of the Bloodgood, the Julienne, the Tyson, the Moyamensing, the Washington, the Bartlett, the Marie Louise, the Duchesse d'Angouleme, the Chaumontel, or the Seckel, among pears. All these, and numerous other varieties, are to be traced to the same cause: at first to "accident," and then to culture and propagation. No man can *demonstrate* that the varieties in the human species *may* not have been produced under some such law, by an origin which can no more be accounted for than the origin of the Catawba Grape, the Moorpark Apricot, or the Rare-Ripe Peach. It is not affirmed that this *is* the origin of the different races of men; it is affirmed only that the man who maintains that all the varieties of the human race have *not* descended from one pair must demonstrate that a law which prevails so extensively in regard to animals and plants, and which is the foundation of the vast *variety* existing in those kingdoms—a variety *apparently* as great as those which are found in the human species—could NOT have had an existence in the propagation of man. The presumption from analogy would seem to be that this was at least *probable;* the contrary can never be demonstrated.

(3) It is necessary for those who assert that the diversities of the human race cannot be accounted for philosophically on either of the two suppositions which have been referred to, to demonstrate that it cannot have been caused by some direct divine interposition, by which, for some cause not now known to us, such a change may have been produced in the constitution of certain portions of the race as to lay the foundation for the diversities which now exist. That God has had, and still has, the *power* to do this, no one can deny; and whether he ever *has* thus interposed in relation to man, or to any other creatures upon the earth, is a question to be examined, and which is a fair subject of inquiry. A rejecter of revelation has not the right to

assume that this could not be; for changes have occurred on the earth certainly not less remarkable, or less difficult of explanation, than this would be. A great change of belief has already commenced, and will be likely to extend much farther than it has yet done, in regard to the divine interposition in the affairs of the earth. Formerly the whole doctrine of miracles was denied, and the denial was attempted to be maintained on the ground of science. It was held to be unphilosophical to suppose that God would interpose in any such way as to change, or, as it was expressed, 'to violate' the laws of nature; and Mr. Hume endeavored to demonstrate that it was impossible to be proved by human testimony that any such changes have occurred. One of the great revolutions produced by the disclosures of geology consists in the fact that God is again introduced into his own world, and in the demonstration of the fact, that he has, from time to time, interposed in the affairs of the earth by a succession of most remarkable *miracles*—that is, by producing changes which cannot be traced to any secondary antecedent causes, or to the operation of mere physical laws. It is now established by the disclosures of geology that there has been on the earth a succession of races of animals, a large part of which have passed away, and that these successive races came upon the earth, not by *development* from some anterior and inferior race, but by a *beginning*—a springing into existence anew—a *creation*—and therefore a *miracle.* No conclusion of geology is more clear and well defined than this, that those races are distinct from each other; that one is not a development from a preceding race; that they have *begun* to be, and that having accomplished their purpose, they have passed away to give place to a *new* race or order of higher character, and better adapted to the new condition of the world, until at last *man* appeared, not as a development from an inferior race, but as a new form of being. Now, these new and successive races of animals must either have been the production of physical laws, or must have sprung up by "spontaneous generation," or must have been developed from an inferior race, or must have been brought upon the stage by direct creative power. The science of geology, left to itself, has set aside each of the former of these suppositions, and has disclosed to the world the fact that there have been successive CREATIONS upon the earth, occupying vast periods of duration, perhaps millions of years, until the whole was crowned by the *creation* of man; and that, so far from its being true that *miracles* are impossible, nothing has been more common on the earth. God has been continually interposing by miraculous creative power. Each new order of beings that has been introduced into the world, has been brought upon the stage by a *miracle;* each new act of creation has been a *miracle;* and whatever may have been, in the estimation of Mr. Hume, the insufficiency of "*human* testimony," in establishing a miracle, no one can doubt now the "testimony" of geology, as found in the fossil remains of the extinct generations of beings scattered over the earth, each followed by a new creation, that there have been interventions of Divine power above that of any existing "laws of nature," in producing momentous changes in the affairs of our world; that is, that miracles "have been matters of quite common occurrence," for every act of *creation* must be a miracle.

It is not, therefore, an opinion which should be set aside as unworthy of attention, that God *may* have interposed at some period, or periods, in the affairs of men, in producing changes in the human condition which would account for all the diversities now found among the races of men upon the earth.

The remark which I have been now making is, that we have a right to demand that he who denies the truth of the Scripture statement that the race is made of one blood, and is descended from one pair, should be able to set aside *each* of these suppositions, before he can philosophically reject the testimony of the Bible on the subject. If *either* of these suppositions will account for the varieties in the human race, or, if *either* of them *may* have occurred—that is, if it is impossible to demonstrate that they could *not* have occurred, then it is not unphilosophical to receive the testimony of the Bible in the case as true.

The opinion of the writer of this Essay would be of no value as to the question *which* of these three suppositions is most philosophical, and which will ultimately be found to be true; but I may be permitted to submit the inquiry whether the *second* of those suggested, and which has not been commonly referred to in endeavoring to account for the diversities of the race, will not be found to be most in accordance with the analogies of nature. The believer in the Bible must suppose that the solution is to be found in one of them, and he may be held to the responsibility of showing that *one* of them is probable and philosophical. It is indispensable for the rejecter of revelation to show that *neither* of them can possibly be true.

CHAPTER IV.

CONCLUSION. WHAT IS THE FOUNDATION OF FAITH IN THE WORD OF GOD.

THE conclusions which have been reached in this Essay, if the reasoning which has been pursued is sound, are the following:—

(1) That there is in the nature of things such a thing as truth—as right and wrong; such a thing as justice, benevolence, holiness, in themselves considered, and without reference to any power ordaining them to be such. God is holy, not simply because he is what he *is*, and because he chooses to call *this* holiness, or because he requires his creatures to believe that what he chooses *to be* constitutes holiness, but because there is such a thing as holiness in itself, and because *that* holiness is found in him. The opposite of this would not be holiness, even if found in God, and if he chose to require that it should be regarded as holiness. So God is true; God is just; God is good, not simply because certain attributes exist in him and he choose to *call* those attributes truth, justice, and goodness, but because there *is* such a thing as truth, justice, goodness in the nature of things, and because these things are found in fact in the essential nature of God. The opposite of these things would *not* be truth, justice,

goodness, even if found in God, and even if he should solemnly *require* that they should be regarded *as* such. God is thus worthy of adoration, confidence, love, not because he has chosen to *possess* certain attributes and to *call* them holiness, truth, justice, and goodness, but because his nature is, in fact, and apart from any arbitrary appointment, holy, true, just, and good. His nature is perfect, not simply because it is what it is, and he choose to *call* it perfection because it is his, but because there *is* such a thing as a perfect character; and that character is found in him. Any supposable change of his nature; any act by which he would become different from what he is, would not make that *new* nature perfect or holy because it was his, and because he chose that it should be regarded as perfect; but if he became what we now regard as unjust, untrue, and malevolent, it *would* be injustice, falsehood, and malevolence still, though it were found in him. We adore, love, and reverence God not because he has *made* one thing true and another false, and required us to regard it as such *because* he has so made them, but because he *is* holy, just, good, and true, and is, in fact, worthy of universal adoration and praise. The foundation of our faith in him is that he *is* a perfect Being; not that he is an arbitrary Being, a Being of mere power, that *can* "call evil good or good evil," and thus require his creatures to adopt a shifting morality at his pleasure.

(2) The nature of God is such that it, in fact, corresponds with that which is eternally true, good, just, and right, or that it *represents* that and *measures* that. His character, his laws, his plans, always correspond with, and represent that which is eternally right.

Knowing what his character is, or what his will is, we know what is right and what is wrong; for he expresses and represents that in his whole nature and in all his laws. We need no other standard of right and wrong, of truth and error, therefore, than his will, for that will corresponds with what is eternally right and just; we are sure that, when we understand his nature and his will, we understand what is eternally just, true, and good. Thus his character and his will become the exponent or measure of what is just and true, not because he *makes* one thing to be true and another false, one thing good and another evil, by an act of will, but because such is the perfection of his nature that it cannot be otherwise than that it should represent and express what is best. Man is so made that, when his mind acts freely and under right influences, he regards his Maker as perfect. God designed, in forming the human soul, that it should be so made as to attribute perfection to its Creator, and to have confidence in him *as* a perfect Being. The soul of man was so made by a clear purpose on the part of the Creator, and the skill and wisdom of the Creator have been eminently shown in making it thus.

In accordance with this view, we are led to believe that the universe is MADE with the highest wisdom and goodness. It is not merely formed in a certain way, and *pronounced* to be good and wise because it is the mere pleasure of God that it should be so regarded, and because he *chooses* that what he has done should be regarded as wise and good, but it is made as it would be on the supposition that it was intended to make a world that should develop what *is* wise and good. The human frame is made in the best manner for the ends contemplated, not because it is made in a certain way and then *pronounced* to be made in the best manner, or because God requires us to believe that what he does is best simply because he chooses to call it so, but because it *is* wisely and skilfully made. It is made as one *would* make it who should undertake to adapt it perfectly to the ends in view. So in the vegetable kingdoms; so in the mineral kingdoms; so in the air, the water, the land; so in the universe of stars and suns. The whole framework of nature *is* thus wisely fitted up; and the proper result of the study of the works of God is not merely to learn what he has *done*, and then to *call* that wisdom and goodness because *he* has chosen to call it so, but to learn through those works that God *is* wise, and great, and good, and just. The universe is made just as it *would be made* by a Being of infinite wisdom, goodness, and, therefore, it is made in the best manner possible. God is to be adored and loved, not because he made a universe without any regard to what was wise and best, and then chose that we should regard what he had done as wise and best; but he is to be adored and loved because he has done all things in conformity with the most perfect idea of what *is* wise and best, and he is, THEREFORE, a Being who is worthy of universal confidence and love.

Hence men 'study nature;' learning from nature not merely what God *does*, but what is *best*. They find there not only the wisest arrangements, but the wisest models for them to imitate. Most of the mechanical contrivances among men are mere imitations of nature, because God has done there what it is *best* and *wisest* to be done. He understood the case perfectly, and he adapted his arrangements to what *is* wisest and best. In the mechanic arts; in the structure of ships, houses, bridges, arches; in relation to the power of the lever, the screw, the inclined plane—to lifting weights, and to locomotion—men are learning more and more to abandon their own models and to study those of nature; and in these explorations of nature, men are rapidly coming to the conclusion that in reference to *any* object which they may desire to accomplish, they may find somewhere in nature a more perfect *model* than they can themselves devise, and that all that they can hope to do is to approximate it in some humble degree, but with no hope of being able to form one *as* perfect themselves. The most perfect models for ships, for example, are found in nature, and the perfection of naval architecture is closely connected with an acquaintance with the form and structure of the fishes and fowls whose home is the water, and which are made to glide safely on the water or swiftly through it.

Geology, while it has seemed to endanger revelation, has also contributed much to a correct knowledge of God, and of his truth. Among other things, it has shown how accurately the principle now referred to was consulted even in the structure of those animals that have now passed away, for even in what are now regarded as the humblest forms of animal life—forms of life of so little consequence in the great scale of being that they have been suffered forever to pass away—proofs of skill are found such as now enter into the highest mechanical contrivances. God made things good not by an arbitrary decree, or, in other words, they were not good because he simply *made* them, but made them as perfect as they could be, according to the best idea of what was demanded in the circumstances. The most ingenious contrivances of men have been in numerous cases anticipated, and are but a "repetition of a previously executed design." "The partitions," for example, "which separate into chambers all the whorls of the ammonite except the outermost one, were exquisitely adapted to strengthen, by the tortuous windings of their outer edges, a shell which had to combine great lightness with great powers of resistance. Itself a continuous arch throughout, it was supported by a series of arches inside, somewhat resembling in form the groined ribs of the Gothic roof, but which, unlike the ponderous stonework of the mediæval architects, were as light as they were strong. And to this combination of arches there was added, in the ribs and grooves of the cell, yet another element of strength —that which has of late been introduced into iron roofs, which, by means of their corrugations—ribs and grooves like those of the ammonite—are made to span over wide spaces, without the support of beams or rafters. Still more recently the same principle has been introduced into metallic boats, which, when corrugated, like the old ammonites, are found to be sufficiently strong to resist almost any degree of pressure without the wonted addition of an exterior framework. The belemnite seems to have united the principle of the float to that of the sinker, as we see both of them united in some of our modern life-boats, which are preserved on their keel by one principle, and preserved from foundering by another. The trilobites were covered over back and head with the most exquisitely constructed plate armor; but as their abdomens seem to have been soft and defenceless, they had the ability of coiling themselves round on the approach of danger, plate moving on plate with the nicest adjustment, till the rim of the armed tail rested on that of the armed head, and the creature presented the appearance of a ball defended at every point. Nor were the ancient crinoids less remarkable for the amount of nice contrivance which their structures exhibited, than the ancient molluscs or crustaceans. In their calyx-like bodies, consisting always of many parts, we find the principle of the arch introduced in almost every possible form and modification, and the utmost flexibility secured to their stony arms by the amazing number of the pieces of which they were composed, and the nice disposition of the joints. The bony scales which covered fishes such as the Osteolepis and Diplopterus of the Old Red Sandstone, were of considerable mass and thickness. They could not, compatibly with much nicety of finish, be laid over each other, like the thin horny scales of the salmon or herring; and so we find them curiously fitted together, not like slates on a modern roof, but like hewn stones on an ancient one. There ran on the upper surface of each, along the anterior side and higher end, a groove of a depth equal to half the thickness of the scale; and along the posterior side and lower end, on the under surface, a sort of bevelled chamber, which, fitting into the grooves of the scales immediately behind and beneath it, brought their surfaces to the same line, and rendered the shining coverings of these strongly armed ganoids as smooth and even as those of the most delicately coated fishes of the present day."—*Testimony of the Rocks.* By Hugh Miller, pp. 241–247.

The world is full of contrivances of this sort, tending to illustrate the idea that the Great Creator is a Being of infinite *wisdom* and *goodness*, and that things are made in accordance with what is *in itself* wise and good. There is nothing arbitrary in those works. The arrangements are resorted to not as a matter of mere *will*, but because it is *best* that they should be resorted to.

The idea here suggested, and which it has been the object of this Essay to illustrate, is, that the nature of God is such that his character is perfectly conformed to what *is* right and best. In all things his will is best, not simply because it *is* his will, but because it is *in itself* best, and because such is his nature that what He does *is* always conformed to that.

Thus, we have confidence in God: not as a Being of mere power; not as one who does what he pleases and then ordains that what he does is best, simply because he wills it; not as one who might have willed or done the opposite of what he has willed and done, and who then, with equal ease, could have made *that* right by an act of will; not as one who calls one thing evil and another good because he chooses to do so, and who might have reversed the arrangement if he had chosen to do it; not as one who has made us simply to approve of what *he* has done, and who could have made us to have approved the reverse if he had chosen to do so; not as one who has shaped the conscience merely to approve of what he *does*, irrespective of the question whether it is right or wrong, and who might, if he had chosen, have so made the conscience as to approve of what it now condemns, and to feel pain at what now gives it pleasure. Not for reasons such as these have we confidence in God, and not for reasons such as these are we required to have confidence in him, but his nature is *worthy* of confidence, because he *is* good, and true, and holy; because his will is always conformed to what *is* just and right; because he has so made us that we *can* be virtuous after his own image, that we *can* approve of what is right in itself, that we can be prompted by our conscience to what is in itself good, that we can be deterred from what is evil because a certain course *is* evil, that we can be led in a path which is straight and right because it *is* straight and right. In one word, God is not an arbitrary being, sporting with right and wrong; giving arbitrary names to things; exalting things indifferent into virtues, or making things that are harmless, vices; making things good or evil at his will; establishing by mere will a temporary and flexible morality: he is a Being all whose words, and laws, and commands, and acts are conformed to what IS ETERNALLY AND UNCHANGEABLY RIGHT. It is only in such a Being that we can have confidence; only under the government of such a God that the interests of the universe can be secure. Knowing, if we can in any way, what *is* true and right, we know what God will do and ordain; knowing, in any way, what he does, and what he ordains, we know that *that* is right, for his nature is such that *that* result will always be secured. The foundation of our confidence, then, in God is that his nature *is absolutely perfect;* that it is conformed to what is eternally true, and just, and good, and holy, and best.

(3) The foundation of faith in his word, therefore, is, that that word is the expression of what *he* sees to be true and right, and that, therefore, it is worthy of our confidence in the same way that he himself is. It is based on evidence that it is indeed his word, and though in all cases we may not be able to see its reasonableness

—as we cannot in all cases see the reason of his doings—yet we feel assured that his word has a foundation *in the truth itself*, as his doings have a foundation *in wisdom.* In neither case do we contemplate a mere utterance of will, but we contemplate what we are made to regard as wisdom and truth. The faith which we have in his word is faith in himself, and resolves itself ultimately into that. It is a confident belief that what he reveals *is* in accordance with what is eternally true and right. If it be supposed that he would make a revelation at all, he could communicate as truth nothing else than what he has communicated. He could not, by an act of will, have made to be true the reverse of those things which he has now revealed as true, nor could he have made those things to be right which would be the reverse of what he has now commanded. As he could not have made two and two seven, or the three angles of a triangle more than two right angles, so he could not have made ingratitude, pride, selfishness, dishonesty, fraud, oppression, cruelty, slavery, right. There are eternal principles of truth and justice. He has made us to approve of those principles, and to disapprove of the opposite; and he has made us to love and reverence *him* because all his acts and laws are conformable to those principles. We could not approve the conduct or love the character of a God whose revealed word was not conformed to these eternal principles.

(4) In those matters, which lie level to our comprehension, or within the limits of our present faculties, his revealed truth *commends* itself to our understandings and our consciences, in such a way that we *perceive* it to be true. We might not have been able to discover it ourselves. The human mind might never have *come*

up to it in its onward progress. But when it *is* revealed, it commends itself as true, and we receive it as such. We see that it accords with all our convictions of truth; with all the principles of our nature; with all the demands of our moral and intellectual being; with all the circumstances of our condition; with all our constitutional desires and aspirations. The doctrines which he has revealed commend themselves to us in such a sense that the opposite could *not* be made to commend themselves to us, or so that we could *not* find in our being that which would approve of the opposite of these things as true. As no revelation could so present the proposition that all the angles of a triangle are *greater* than two right angles that we could receive it as true, so there are propositions in morals and religion which could *not* be so commended to us by any pretended revelation that we could possibly receive them as true. They would be false to our nature; false to our instincts; false to our hopes; false to our experience; false to the whole course of things on earth. We could *not*, by any authority of a pretended revelation, be made to embrace the proposition that intemperance is a virtue, for the whole course of things is against such a proposition. No virtue *could* lead to such results as intemperance does. We could not, by any pretended revelation, be made to believe that ingratitude, falsehood, treachery, dishonesty, theft, oppression, are virtues; for all the instincts of our nature, all the laws of our being, all the results of conduct, demonstrate to us that such things cannot be virtues. But we can believe, we do easily believe, that the conduct recommended in the golden rule is virtuous; for, although we might not have been able to originate that rule ourselves, it so commends itself to us when it *is* revealed that we see at once that it is right and good. The same is true of the requirements of honesty, fidelity, kindness, benevolence, charity, and chastity. The same is true of the law which requires us to pray, to love God, to keep his law, to lead a serious life, to prepare for another world. Nothing could convince the world at large that theft and piracy are right; nothing can convince the world at large that slavery is right; and if in a book of pretended revelation these things were sanctioned as right, or enjoined as just, the book would ultimately be rejected by mankind. Man could not be convinced that such a book came from God—for such doctrines are opposed to the constitution of our nature, and they cannot be embraced by the world as right.

It is the fact now adverted to which is the foundation of the strong attachment of Christians to the truths of the Bible. They *see* the statements in the Bible to be true. These statements accord with all the demands of their nature; with all the wants of their condition; with all their own experience; with all the circumstances of their being. Nothing can convince them that the religion which reveals such truths is false. They may not be able to demonstrate, so as to meet the cavils of objectors, that the miracles alleged to have been wrought, were wrought; they may not be qualified to enter into the learned questions which arise in regard to the criticism of the sacred books; they may be unable to meet many of the sneers and cavils of infidels; but they are assured that the truths in the Bible accord with the wants of their nature, and are such as it is proper that a revelation should communicate to mankind. They are so made that they *cannot* believe those statements to be false. No terror of the flames of martyrdom can convince them that they are not true. Euclid could never have been convinced that two rectangles, which have the same altitude, are not to each other as their bases; Pythagoras could never have been convinced that in a right-angled triangle the square of the hypothenuse is *not* equal to the sum of the squares of the two sides; and Galileo, with all his submission to the authority of the church, never *was* convinced that the Copernican system of astronomy is not the true system. No fury of persecution; no terrors of the rack, the thumb-screw, the fagot, ever could have convinced those men that they did not hold the truth on those subjects. In like manner, no terror of the rack or the stake can convince a Christian that he has not by nature a sinful heart; that he is not bound to love God; that the law of God is not such as his conscience and reason approve; that the plan of salvation is not adapted to his wants as a sinner, as a dying man, and as a traveller to another world. Nothing can convince him that the requirements of the Gospel are not adapted to promote his own purity, peace, and happiness, or that that Gospel would not put a period to the evils that now reign upon the earth. The Gospel commends itself to his nature; it meets his wants; it satisfies his soul; it fills him with peace; it sustains him in trial; it aids him in the hour of temptation; it inspires him with hope; it elevates his character, and imparts to him a joy which he has sought in vain in the pleasures and pursuits of the world. He may not be able to 'argue' for these truths, but he can 'burn' for them; and hence thousands and tens of thousands of Christians, many of them 'unlearned and ignorant'—many of them trained in the refinements of elevated life—many of them tender and delicate females—have gone cheerfully to the stake in attestation of their faith in the Redeemer.

(5) In matters which lie beyond the limits of our reason, the precepts of a true revelation will be in the range of truths already known, and will commend themselves to us as such. We have the same confidence in the disclosures of the telescope which we have in those which are made by the naked eye. We as really believe in the existence of Uranus or Neptune; in the existence of stars in the various nebulæ; and in the existence of the asteroids between Mars and Jupiter, as we do in the sun or the moon. The foundation of faith is the same; and a man will as certainly and confidently act on the belief of the one as the other. So in regard to the truths of revelation. Many of those truths could never have been discovered by the unaided reason of man. But they lie in the range of truths already known, and none of them are contradictory to truths with which we are familiar, and on which we act from day to day. The instrument by which they are communicated to us makes no difference in regard to the foundation or the strength of our faith, any more than the fact that one object is made known to us by the naked eye and another by the telescope makes a difference in the foundation of our faith in natural things. The foundation of faith in either case is simply that what is believed is TRUE. It matters not *how* the truth in the case is communicated to the mind; the fact that it IS true is that on which the mind relies. In the cases just supposed, we rely in one instance on the testimony of the naked eye, in another on the testimony of the telescope; in

either case, on our conviction that what is believed is *true.* In matters pertaining to God; to the atonement; to the resurrection of the dead; to the realities of another world, we rest on the conviction of our own reason and conscience as far as they will carry us, and then on the testimony of God in matters above our reason: in either case on the belief that what is embraced by the mind is *true.* Our faith then in those things which lie beyond the limits of our own immediate observation is of the same nature, and is as firm, as in respect to those things which *are* within the range of our unaided powers, as faith in the revelations of the telescope is of the same nature as faith in the disclosures made by the naked eye.

(6) From the nature of the case, and from the results of all the progress that man has made thus far in science, the friend of the Bible may and should believe that all the disclosures yet to be made in science will be in accordance with the teachings of that book. As the teachings of the Bible commend themselves to our reason; to the instincts of our nature; to all just conceptions of right and wrong; to the eternal doctrines of truth; to all our wants and to all our hopes—as they accord with what science has disclosed thus far, and as the results have shown that there may be just confidence in the Bible so far as the knowledge of man has gone, the friend of the Bible is justified in supposing that it will always be so. The Bible, in its moral teachings, has commended itself to mankind as being in accordance with the principles of eternal truth and justice; it has kept in advance on the subject of morals of all that man could discover from other sources, and is still in advance; science has not yet disclosed anything that has been

demonstrated to be contradictory to the statements of the Bible; the results of all the discoveries made have been only to extend the conviction in the world that the Bible is true, and as the Bible occupies this position in an age of the world such as this is, it cannot be regarded as an unjustifiable anticipation that it will always occupy a similar position. The believer in the Bible has nothing to fear. The just foundation of faith in the word of God has not thus far been shaken. From this point, it seems to be proper that the believer in the book should look onward without apprehension of the future. The chemist *will* conduct his inquiries in accordance with the laws of his own science, and without reference to the questions of exegesis about the meaning of the Bible, or of any other book. Let him do it. Let him not be disturbed in his communion with retorts, and blowpipes, and crucibles, even though he should pursue his inquiries with the feelings of Mephistopheles in Faust.—The miner will dig in the rocks, will turn up again the old foundations of the earth, and pursue his inquiries amidst the monuments of by-gone ages—the relics and memorials of extinct generations of animals—the monuments that tell of modes of being that have long since passed away, and that are now unknown—quite irrespective of any inquiry about what the Bible teaches respecting the age of the world. Let him do it. Let him not be disturbed as he wields his pick-axe, by any of the questions which interpreters of the Bible have raised about the meaning of the first chapter of Genesis. Thus far the result has shown that from such sources the friend of the Bible has nothing to fear.—The astronomer will point his glass to the heavens, and search for new stars, planets, comets, asteroids; will endeavor to resolve the still unresolved nebulæ, and to bring other nebulæ into view, to be resolved in turn by some future explorer, and he will do all this with no reference as to what the Bible teaches on the subject of creation. Let him do it. Thus far the friend of the Bible has had nothing to fear from these discoveries, and he has no ground to apprehend the result of any disclosures which astronomy may have yet to make.—The antiquarian will brush the dust from ancient monuments, and seek to decipher the meaning of long-buried inscriptions on temples and tombs; and he will do this with no reference to what the Bible teaches as to the antiquity of the human race. Let him do it. Thus far the friend of the Bible has seen no reason for apprehension as to the result of such inquiries. Champollion and Lepsius in Egypt, and Layard in Assyria, have done nothing to shake the confidence of the Christian in the Bible; and it is not an unfair anticipation that no future disclosures from ancient tombs and temples will shake the foundation of faith in the word of God. And so the race will make progress in morals; in political science; in the refinements and courtesies of domestic and public intercourse; in the promptings of humanity; in the impulses of a generous benevolence; in its views of what is proper in the dealings of man with man; in the claims to liberty as a right to be enjoyed by all men—but in none of these things will mankind ever get in advance of the teachings of the word of God. These teachings are in accordance with eternal truth; and the nearer the approximation which men make in any form of knowledge to the principles of eternal truth, the more will they appreciate and love the word of God. The farther they advance in that knowledge, also, the more will they venerate the character of God—for they will but perceive more clearly that that character is not arbitrary—is not changeable—is not founded on a mere purpose of will—but that it is in accordance with what is eternally true, and right, and wise, and good; that he is to be adored because his nature is so perfect that all that he says and does will be in accordance with what is best, and will in all things be the exact *measure* of what is true and good.

The sum of all—the result of all our inquiries is this: The foundation of faith in God and in his word is, that GOD IS INFINITELY WISE, JUST, AND GOOD; not that he is an arbitrary Being, making evil good and good evil at his pleasure; not as having the right to reverse these things if he should choose; not as having the power of making that right which is now wrong, or that wrong which is now right—that true which is now false, or that false which is now true—that crooked which is now straight, or that straight which is now crooked—that benevolent which is now malignant, and that malignant which is now benevolent; but the foundation of confidence in God and his word is in the fact that there is an eternal distinction between right and wrong—that there are things that are right in themselves, and things that are wrong in themselves—and that the character of God IS SO PERFECT THAT ALL THAT HE SAYS AND DOES IS, AND WILL EVER BE, IN ACCORDANCE WITH WHAT IS ETERNALLY TRUE, AND RIGHT, AND BEST.

THE END.

www.ingramcontent.com/pod-product-compliance
Lightning Source LLC
LaVergne TN
LVHW011234110826
845150LV00006B/1636

* 9 7 8 1 4 2 5 5 1 3 9 2 4 *